MANAGING CHANGE:
Today's Challenge to Management

MANAGING CHANGE:
Today's Challenge to Management

JOHN E. FLAHERTY

NELLEN PUBLISHING COMPANY, Inc.
NEW YORK

Library of Congress Cataloging in Publication Data

Flaherty, John E
 Managing change.
 Bibliography: p.
 Includes index.
 1. Entrepreneur. 2. Organizational change.
I. Title.
HB601.F53 658.4'06 78-4179
ISBN 0-8424-0115-6

Copyright © 1979, by Nellen Publishing Company, Inc.

All rights reserved. No part of this work covered by the copyright hereon may be reproduced or used in any form or by any means—graphic, electronic, mechanical, including photocopying, recording, taping, or information storage and retrieval systems—without permission of the publisher.

NELLEN PUBLISHING COMPANY · INC.
386 PARK AVENUE SOUTH · NEW YORK · N.Y. 10016 212 · 679 · 0937

To

CHRISTINE

CONTENTS

Chapter	Page
I. CHANGE AND ENTREPRENEURSHIP	1
Business and Change	2
Social Significance	4
II. ENTREPRENEURSHIP	9
Contributions of the Academic Field	10
Economic Theory	10
Economic History	14
Management Theory	14
The Entrepreneurship Personality	15
The Role of Creativity	16
The Benavioral and Social Sciences	17
Organizational Restraints	17
The Concepts of Uncertainty, Profit, Risk and Opportunity	19
Uncertainty	19
Profit Myopia	23
Profit and Profitability	24
Stress on Owner-Orientation	24
Restricted Scope of Business Activity	25
Limited Time Horizon	26
Neglect of Future Costs and Benefits	26
Creation of Public Hostility	26
Misplaced Emphasis on the Profit Motive	27
Profitability	27
Risk and Opportunity	29
Boehm-Bawork's Theorem	29
A New Business Versus Ongoing Business Risks	30
Entrepreneurship as a Process	31
Ambiguity of Risk	31
Risk and Opportunity Characteristics	32
Categories of Risk and Opportunity	34
III. APPROACHES TO ENTREPRENEURIAL STRATEGIES	37
Continuity and Change	39
Illustration of Corporate Change— Sears' Strategic Decisions	42

Chapter	Page
The Traditional Business	43
The Claims of the Past	43
Complacency of Success	44
Planning Need	45
Power of Tradition	45
Defining the Business—Quest for Corporate Identity	46
The Mirage of Product Definition	47
The Concept of Knowledge Excellence	48
The Mystique of Success	50
Need for Increasing Effectiveness of Traditional Business	51
The Transitional Business	52
Challenge of New Commitments	52
Dynamic Tensions of Becoming	52
Chief Task—Focus on New Opportunities	52
Coping With Uncertainty—Techniques	54
Statistical Forecasting	54
Futurology	54
Weakness of Futurology	56
Future—What We Know About It For Certain	56
Testing Underlying Assumptions	56
Management's Perception of Environment Determines Direction	57
Environmental Restraints	58
Knowledge as Protection Against Surprise	58
Role of Anticipation	59
The Recent Past—Projection	59
Environmental Audit	59
The Transformational Business	62
Admission of Ignorance—A Prerequisite	62
Organizing Ignorance	62
Purposefully Planned Change	63
What Should Our Business Be?	64
The AT&T Story	67
IV. ENTREPRENEURIAL TACTICS	73
Introduction	73
Anheuser's Answer to "What Is Our Business"	74
Diagnostic Tools	75
Pareto's Law of Social Distribution	76
Cost and Revenue Streams—The Transaction Analysis	79

Chapter	Page
The Mirage of Planned Obsolescence	82
Abandonment	85
Concentration	87
Vulnerability Analysis	90
Marketing and Managerial Guidelines	93
The Competitive Environment	93
Life Cycle Analysis	96
Segmentation	99
Financial Planning	101
The People Area	104
External Resources	104
V. APPROACHES TO MANAGERIAL EFFECTIVENESS	107
Introduction	107
Organizational and Behavioral Theory	107
The Guerrilla Fighters	109
The Cynics	109
Motivation	110
Definition	110
Interpretations	111
Recent Thinkers	113
Conclusion	121
VI. THE ENTREPRENEURIAL EXECUTIVE	125
Introduction	125
Managerial Literacy	125
Managing Knowledge Work	126
Positioning for Entrepreneurial Effectiveness	127
The Strategy Stance	127
The Managerial Climate	131
The Quest for Entrepreneurial Effectiveness	138
Footnotes	153
Bibliography	161
Index	**167**

ACKNOWLEDGEMENT

THE impetus for this study grew out of two main roots, one pragmatic and the other inspirational. In preparing a new multidisciplinary course on the Entrepreneurial Process for the Pace University doctoral program, I was compelled to review the literature in the field in order to obtain a systematic synthesis.

On the inspirational side, I am especially indebted to Peter Drucker. The entrepreneurial approach to the management of change has been a central common denominator of his many works on business management. Several years ago he personally triggered my interest in organizing the subject matter into a more meaningful whole. His many insights have been invaluable, but his friendly encouragement in urging me to complete the task has been even more important. Avid followers of Drucker will immediately recognize my tremendous intellectual debt to his pioneering research over the years. It is not my intention to improve on Drucker in the entrepreneurial area, but by combining many of his central themes against the backdrop of additional literature in the field, perhaps I have reinforced him in some small way. In any event, it goes without saying that Drucker is in no way responsible for the interpretation and conclusions which are my own.

A number of other individuals deserve a note of thanks. I am grateful to several of my Pace colleagues, Dr. Richard Matthews and Dr. Thomas P. Robinson, for their suggestions in reading initial drafts, and to Mr. John Gibbons for several of his examples which were incorporated into the text. Finally, a note of appreciation is in order to the stimulation I received from the students in my seminar, the typing help from Mrs. Joanne Foglia, and the general research assistance from Mr. Robert Singer, a Pace graduate student.

Preface

The purpose of the book is to explore entrepreneurship on both a theoretical and pragmatic basis. I do not offer a grand resolution to the challenge of entrepreneurship. What I propose is not *the* approach; it is *an* approach to the management of change. Study is divided into three main sections.

The first segment deals with the shortcomings and some contributions of economic theory. It points out that classical economics in postulating a condition of general equilibrium assumed a model in which all economic activity was essentially repetitive, with continuity as the norm. The premises of entrepreneurship, on the other hand, dictate the allocating of resources to future expectations, inferring that change is built into the system—and that continuity is the exception.

Outside the mainstream of classical economic thought, however, a number of thinkers (J.B. Say, Joseph Schumpeter, to cite just two), attempted to bridge the gap between theory and reality. In general, they pointed out that in the real world businessmen in following their entrepreneurial initiative were contributing to economic growth, providing new goods, and creating jobs. In short, we had entrepreneurial practice before we had anything approximating a theory.

The pioneers of entrepreneurial theory noted that classical economics in assuming perfect knowledge failed to take into account such qualitative elements as: uncertainty, risk, the dynamic role of profits, and opportunity. In their writings, the early thinkers captured the spirit of entrepreneurship's two main themes—the shifting of resources from less productive to more productive activities and the allocation of existing resources to future opportunities. Although falling short of any ideal theory, scholars in the field of entrepreneurship have provided a legacy of insights and established the core of knowledge for understanding the discipline.

The beginning portion of the book also covers the relationships of the disciplines of economic history, management theory and the behavioral sciences to the field of entrepreneurship. Finally it concludes with a brief treatment of the concepts of profit, uncertainty, risk and opportunity.

The middle section of the study will concentrate on how the entrepreneurial process is organized with particular emphasis on strategies and tactics. The former suggests a pattern of understanding corporate change by looking at planning in three business dimensions—the traditional, the transitional, and the transformational. The traditional or operational business emphasizes continuity by raising the question: "What is our business?" The transitional or adaptive business stresses adjustment to the short range future in addressing itself to the question: "What will our business be?" The transformational or innovative business focuses on purposefully planned change by introducing the question: "What should our business be?" All three dimensions are interrelated and share the common denominator of centering on the customer's value system and special corporate knowledge strengths. The reality of tactics throughout the study focuses on a number of diagnostic tools, combined with managerial and marketing guidelines, as a possible operating methodology for achieving improved economic results.

A few words of reservation are in order on the proposed strategies and tactics. Modern management has become increasingly cognizant of the need to manage change, but it also realizes the increasing difficulty of effecting change. Entrepreneurship is the best approach available; but at the same time, in dealing with the future and uncertainty, it is bound to remain an elusive discipline. As Walter Lippman once reminded us: "The movement of events is almost always a great deal faster than the movement of our minds." The world of accelerated change is one in which nothing stands still. Although managing change systematically has the advantage of flying by the seat of one's pants, success is never guaranteed. The main contribution of theory is that it adds to our understanding by providing a more systematic way of doing things. Entrepreneurship, the systematic planning for the future needs of society, means dealing with a world incapable of being fully grasped, recognizing that no single perception can capture the whole of reality, and being alert to unexpected and inevitable discontinuities in society. The elder Von Moltke, when chief of staff of the Prussian Army, cautioned about the hubris of certainty in planning when he said: "no plan can survive the test of battle."

Nor do the tactical diagnostic tools lay any claim to precision. Essentially they are early warning sensing mechanisms enabling management to overcome or at least moderate existing operating restraints. Their practicality depends on the situation and the skills of the user. Although they lack the validity of the scientific method, the diagnostic tools are useful in raising the right questions of resource misallocation and having probability work to the possible advantage of the entrepreneur. The use of the tools is based on the assumption that it is possible to learn from successful businesses, making it unnecessary to rediscover America over and over again. In short, it is only when you systematize from theory and experience that you get results, realizing that because existing resources will always place a restraint on what the manager can do you will never get ideal performance.

The focus of the latter part of the study is on the role of the entrepreneurial executive, the knowledge professional in the corporation responsible for results. A legitimate criticism of managerial practice in the recent past is that it has been over administered and under entrepreneured. Changes in society and corporate requirements are breeding a new type of professional executive who will have to supplement his administrative abilities by meeting the challenge of making his knowledge contribute to future business results. In short, in assuming a greater individual accountability for risk taking in implementing executive tasks, he will also need to develop a greater entrepreneurial spirit.

The old notion of simply relegating entrepreneurship to the man who started the business is no longer adequate, the challenge for tomorrow's executive is to see it as an ongoing business function for all levels of the organization. In order to achieve this spirit of entrepreneurship of focusing on opportunities and shifting resources from less to more productive results, the knowledge professional will have to transcend his specialty by developing the concept of managerial literacy and think through his specific knowledge contributions.

The final chapter, therefore, will attempt to reinforce the entrepreneurial spirit by exploring briefly some of the approaches to executive development, the realities of executive life and an examination of a number of operating guidelines for improved performance. It is not aimed primarily at corporate strategy *per se* which will continue to be the province of top management, but will deal with the problems and opportunities which the typical executive faces in his daily activities.

CHAPTER I

CHANGE AND ENTREPRENEURSHIP

ACCELERATING change is the single most significant feature of our age. Gales of tempestuous change characterize the recent past more than any other force in any previous era in history. Sparing nothing in their cyclonic sweep across society, the violent and volatile winds of rapid change swirl about us with alarming intensity, leaving us battered and unsettled from their ravages, and exposing management to the uncertainties of the new and unfamiliar.

The blasts of social revolutionary change are undermining the foundations of all institutions from the family to the national state, blowing aside value systems which served as moral beacons for centuries, casting the educational establishment into a maelstrom of turmoil and turbulence, uprooting codes of military discipline and legal authority previously considered unassailable, paralyzing the rudders of ships of state into a condition of ungovernable inertia, erasing the established knowledge foundations in traditional disciplines, twisting familiar geographic patterns into novel configurations, converting the conventional wisdom of economic and business theory into anachronisms, wrenching the labor union from its comfortable craft moorings, and creating dangerous imbalances in the world ecological network.

Awed and even possibly intimidated by the volume and the intensity of radical change, many observers conclude that the social upheavals are so piercing, permeating, pervasive and penetrating that the concept of permanence had become outmoded. Without completely rejecting Parmenides, the philosopher of permanence, the fact is that the panorama of swift change forces tradition to melt under the onslaughts of innovation, simplicity to surrender to complexity and steady state stability to yield to the pressures of dynamic disequilibrium.

Without question the velocity of change is the main cause of such current upheavals as: the black revolt, the cybernetic revolution, the crisis in government and politics, the knowledge explosion, the feminist movement, the revolution of rising expectations, the consumer movement, the ecological protest, the ethnic identity crisis, the transformation of organizations, the metamorphosis of the city into megalopolis, the dilution of the work ethic and the vacuum in values. These qualitative discontinuities are major tributaries flowing into the rushing river of irreversible revolutionary change.

BUSINESS AND CHANGE

In a placid and less complex environment, businessmen could afford to adjust in a more leisurely fashion to social forces. In today's society change is no longer the exception but the norm. Because our corporate managers must now respond to an ephemeral world which they do not fully understand, the entrepreneurial task of managing change more systematically will assume critical importance in the coming decade. Entrepreneurship has been a major catalyst of much of the change in modern society, but its impact as a crucial corporate function is not yet fully appreciated. As a result of its risk taking characteristics, management is one of the few disciplines in which change is deliberately fostered.

Most institutions find solace in maintaining the status quo, but business corporations are not allowed the comfort of such a serene policy. The unsentimental marketplace forces management to perform endless economic encores; failures to do so invites the possibility of becoming a business fossil.

As actors and not just spectators in a dynamic economic process, managers have no choice but to operate in the uncertain realm of ceaseless change. Despite its shortcomings and its denunciations from social critics, the modern corporation remains superior to any other alternative on the horizon as the major institutional instrument of change. If the enterprise system fails, however, to cope successfully with change, its very survival is at stake. The Congressional vertical divestiture bill facing the oil industry represents one of many such threats. Oil executives view it as the first step toward ultimate nationalization.

The massive input of new events, the obsolescence of products, the uncertainty of marketing new ones, and the changes in technology result in the loss of equilibrium and in growing instability for the corporate milieu.

As the environment shifts dramatically before their eyes, managers find it more and more difficult to take proper bearings for risk and to develop adequate sensing antennae for opportunity. In struggling with these external issues and operating without raucous rhetoric, businessmen are the silent revolutionaries of our society who, at the same time, must become increasingly responsible for their environmental impacts. Businessmen must accept the challenge not because they innately love change more than others, but because they have no alternative. Managing change is a central task of present day management.

Whether the present generation of corporate leadership will be able to manage change successfully is not foreseeable. Unless, as part of its conceptual tool kit, it possesses the vision to recognize clearly that things will be different tomorrow, the task becomes impossible. Rapid change dictates that managers will increasingly have to shift their stance to marketing and technology, from the inside to the outside of the business. Over the past two generations, the major emphasis of study in the emerging discipline of management has been on the inside of the business. Work was done inside the business (or so it seemed) and was understandable; the inside was measurable and conducive to quantified expressions of results; customers were taken for granted and the knowledge foundations appeared safe. If, however, we properly assume conscious and deliberate choice on the part of the manager in shaping the new environment; then, chance, indifference and apathy toward the environment are no longer adequate. In creating, the manager becomes part of his creation, he must not only take credit for his entrepreneurial accomplishment but must share in the blame of his failures.

Innovations and growth force upon management a new dimension of both legitimacy and responsibility which must transcend the narrow economic purpose of the past. In its recent orchestration of economic change, the leading conductors of the business community have produced many brilliant economic symphonies, but there has been little appreciation in the rising static of accompanying environmental issues as a result of their efforts. In addition to providing material prosperity, American business in the next decade will have to face the entrepreneurial challenge of improving the quality of life by converting the negative impacts into economic opportunities.

The need to recognize the relevance of change becomes more crucial when one bears in mind that all social institutions are nourished from the outside. The internal areas of the business are chiefly characterized by problems, cost, efforts and frictions, all of which are singularly devoid of results. Opportunities and growth for any business depend on converting external trends in the customer and knowledge areas into results. Sheer survival alone for any social institution is a parochial objective; a social institution is evaluated in the long run by its contribution to society. Failure to recognize the task of defining its legitimacy means that a corporation is always vulnerable to being put out of business by society.

SOCIAL SIGNIFICANCE

To be effective, entrepreneurship requires a supportive and encouraging atmosphere. Unless nourished by favorable environmental forces, the enterprise, as well as other social institutions, will not survive. A healthy and strong corporation in a sick society is a contradiction in terms.

Almost all the recent literature presented by social critics of both the left and right mirrors a glum image for the future of the present enterprise system. The general tenor of sociological criticism is that modern management is playing the role of its own grave digger. Among the books echoing this pessimistic theme are the following: Daniel Bell, *The Cultural Contradictions of Capitalism;* Michael Harrington, *Socialism;* John K. Galbraith, *Economics and the Public Purpose;* Henry Fairlie, *The Spoiled Child of The Western World,* George Lodge, *The New American Ideology;* Robert Nisbet, *The Twilight of Authority;* Martin Mayer, *Today and Tomorrow in America;* and Ralph Nader, Mark Green and Joel Seligman, *Taming the Giant Corporation.*[1]

With the exception of the Harrington book, all were published after the summer of 1973. Since that date, virtually no significant social critic has been optimistic about the vitality of entrepreneurship. The confluence of a number of crises in the latter part of 1973 (energy, recession, inflation, New York City, ecology, etc.) has produced a morbidly pessimistic attitude among social commentators.

Bell paradoxically concludes that the combination of business success and resulting social hedonism has debilitated the bourgeois spirit of entrepreneurship. Harrington and Galbraith foresee corporate capitalism undergoing a institutional mutation in the direction of socialism. Fairlie contends that the economic and social problems facing America have resulted in a national loss of nerve. Lodge maintains that the present corporate value system based on Lockean property principles has become anachronistic, suggesting that American business will have to develop a new ideology attuned to modern environmental realities. Nisbet argues that our foundations of authority are rapidly vanishing and that the United States, in order to avoid approaching social anarchy, desperately needs a sense of community. Mayer deplores the excess of expectations from governmental programs and points out the need to revitalize the achievement ethic. Along with calling for more information about corporate activities and the conversion of the board of directors into public trustees, Nader and his associates call for the federal chartering of corporations employing at least 10,000 people or having an annual minimum of $250 million in sales. A common thread running through all the works is the lack of a transcendental ethic which is necessary to restrain centrifugal social forces and moderate self-seeking power on the part of all our institutions.

A most disturbing environmental trend operating against entrepreneurship is the growth of the non-profit sector. At present about 50 percent of the G.N.P. is in the non-profit sector[2], indicating that if the trend continues, political determination of resources will supplement market allocation. The market system is not the answer to everything, but in addition to its superior performance over that of government operations, it has the advantage of creating capital for economic growth. In this respect, even the leftist social democratic economy of Sweden has, as one of its main philosophical premises, the inherent performance advantages of the private sector over the public sector. The adoption of such a policy by American political leadership could reverse the growth of the public sector and open the way toward greater re-privatization of the economy. The present ratio of fifty-fifty between the non-profit and private sectors places an enormous burden on the private sector in raising capital, creating jobs and introducing innovations.

If entrepreneurship is to meet the growing social challenges, it needs a less hostile political climate. What the political direction will be is important, but it is not the whole story. Business leadership will have to assume a new and a different stance, one which will be appropriate to the new dynamic environment. Creating a transcendental ethic is beyond the control of a business institution, but through the avenue of entrepreneurship, the latter can by presenting a stronger case for its own legitimacy make a substantial social contribution. In short, the challenge is: how can the corporation legitimatize the management of change?

The management of corporate change encompasses three major connective tissues: entrepreneurship, the catalyst of change; technological and social innovations, the engines of change; and knowledge, the fuel of change. The successful combination of all three in managing change can establish the foundation of a sound corporate legitimacy—a challenge which will assume increasing importance in the immediate future.

Corporate legitimacy, the approval society bestows on an institution by making its power acceptable, is currently in a state of disarray. The traditional arguments for a corporate legitimacy, such as private property, consumer product acceptance, public opinion, voluntary acceptance by employees, and the legal charter will continue to have some significance; but as post-industrial society matures they will manifest diminishing importance. Future endorsement by society will depend on how entrepreneurial management utilizes its knowledge strengths for technological and social innovation.

Entrepreneurial risk taking judgments, aimed at opportunities and based on the application of knowledge and innovation, will become the main claim of corporate legitimacy. The translation of this novel responsibility, involving real accountability, is derived from management's unique and singular resource—the authority of knowledge. Previous leadership groups throughout history claimed status on the basis of birth, charisma, property, religious roles and military position; but for the first time in history, management, the leadership organ of modern society, places its claim to legitimacy on its intellectual ability to translate concepts into meaningful economic results. Innovative entrepreneurship is, in effect, purposefully planned change. It transcends the traditional function of adaptation, by implying, at least to some extent, that the future can be invented.

Because power must be accountable, no better instrument exists for the justification of power than the entrepreneurial ability to make knowledge effective and innovation successful. If management fails in the task of managing change or abuses its authority, society can remove the power it has granted. In the last several years a substantial amount of disturbing evidence has appeared indicating that management as a leadership organ is not satisfactorily performing its job. According to the public opinion surveys of Daniel Yankelovitch, over ninety-three percent of Americans express their willingness "to make personal sacrifices, if necessary to preserve the free enterprise system." At the same time, Yankelovitch found that only thirty percent of the people have confidence in business leadership.

Why the gap between belief in the institution and distrust of its leadership? Partly it is a result of imperfect knowledge about entrepreneurship. Although the core of a discipline exists, it is also clear that management still has a good deal to learn. The study will stress that at present we need to improve our understanding, add to the conceptual base, and enlarge our vision of entrepreneurship.

Difficult external pressures in the form of intractable social and economic problems along with oppressive governmental regulations have also made the managerial task more difficult, adding to the lack of social approval. Moreover, for more than a generation American management has basked in the sun of outstanding economic performance, resulting in an escalation of social expectations. Now management is standing in the shadows of its past success, but the expectations have not abated.

In the nineteen fifties and the sixties under the guise of social responsibility, many liberals felt that business would come to society's rescue by solving all social problems. In the more sobering seventies it is clear there is a danger if society expects too much and if business attempts to accommodate society by making unrealistic promises; business can only do so much. If business is to maintain its leadership role it cannot neglect the quality of life, but a tradeoff is necessary between social expectations and corporate resources.

But perhaps the most disturbing evidence creating a tainted image of business leadership is the loss of moral quality, a prerequisite of any leadership group. The recent payoff scandals in many sectors of American corporate life have produced one of the most severe indictments in the annals of business. If the moral virtue of integrity is lacking, it will in the long run destroy the greatest economic performance.

Fortunately, a number of sensitive business leaders are aware of the danger. For example, A. W. Clausen, Chairman of the Board of the Bank of America, remarked:

> There has been a massive erosion of public confidence in the integrity of business. It is our job to restore that confidence. . . .As of this moment the public is rightly skeptical of our practices and our preachings. . .integrity is not some impractical notion dreamed up by naive do-gooders. Our integrity is the foundation for, the very basis of our ability to do business. If the market economy ever goes under, our favorite villains—socialist economies and government regulators won't be to blame. We will. If we are not concerned, then we are not sensitive to the reality of the problem in today's world.[3]

Can the enterprise system continue to survive? Yes, if modern management practices its entrepreneurial mission by utilizing its unique knowledge toward the creation of social and technological innovation, while at the same time combining the moral quality of integrity. The challenge is great but that is the responsibility of a leadership group. Meeting the challenge successfully will enhance the corporation's legitimacy.

CHAPTER II

ENTREPRENEURSHIP

INTRODUCTION

MANAGING change for the purpose of achieving economic results is the central challenge facing modern management. Within the framework of an increasingly unstable environment the entrepreneurial task inevitably involves encounters with risk, uncertainty and opportunity. Because the outside elements of a business are always in flux, management must continually adapt, react and quite often innovate to fulfill customer needs, meet new forms of competition, adjust to new societal trends, and finally, to keep abreast of new technology. In short, the entrepreneurial task is essentially twofold: first, improving current business performance by shifting resources from lower to higher levels of productivity; and, second, committing existing resources to the achievement of business growth by systematic risk taking and maximizing opportunities.

The task is not new. Businessmen have always been the silent revolutionaries of economic and social change. At the same time, because businessmen have been so busy practicing entrepreneurship, they have had little opportunity to conceptualize systematically their achievements into a scholarly form. In the academic world a vast literature on entrepreneurship exists, but because it lacks an interdisciplinary focus, theoretical output remains uneven, fragmented and disjointed. Economists, economic historians, management theorists and behavioral scientists have planted entrepreneurial seedlings, but these have not produced a comprehensive theory.

Although it is possible to identify entrepreneurial successes when they occur, entrepreneurship as an organized and systematic process resists facile theorizing. The great value of a theory resides in having a mental road-map of things to be accomplished, combined with appropriate ways of doing them. In short, the critical criterion of any theory is whether it works; at persent no verifiable test for entrepreneurship exists. All we have are a number of practices and insights emerging from successful operations which may serve as the building blocks for some future theory of entrepreneurship. The academic disciplines dealing with entrepreneurship shed only dim light on the landscape and reveal a paucity of relevance. A brief exploration of these scholarly fields will, nevertheless, assist in understanding the current state of the art.

CONTRIBUTIONS FROM THE ACADEMIC FIELD

Economic Theory

The passion of the economics profession for the mental gymnastics of model building has erected two separate economic worlds—the practical one of performance and the theoretical one of the academe. In alluding to the lack of cross-fertilization between the two worlds, Robert Heilbroner, Professor of Economics, New School for Social Research, correctly asserts that "economic theory contributes very little to economic policy." Classical economics has viewed the entrepreneur as a passive agent playing a subsidiary role to the factors of land, labor and capital. A recent study notes the difficulty of incorporating entrepreneurship on a theoretical level into the doctrine of classical economics. Israel Kirzner comments on the impossibility of the entrepreneur's role under conditions of equilibrium.

> In equilibrium there is no room for the entrepreneur. When the decisions of all the market participants dovetail completely so that each plan correctly assumes the corresponding plans of the other participants and no possibility exists for any altered plans that would be simultaneously preferred by the relevant participants, there is nothing left for the entrepreneur to do. He will be unable to discover possibilities from buying from those who underestimated the needs of potential buyers and of their selling to those eager buyers (who in turn have underestimated the eagerness of sellers). Thus, he cannot contribute to the reallocation of resources of products that will overcome inefficiencies and lack of coordination generated by market ignorance, since no such ignorance and lack of coordination exist in equilibrium.[1]

Entrepreneurship

Except for the writings of a handful of economists who will be mentioned in the following pages, entrepreneurship has been a subject of benign neglect. Although the few economists discussing the subject of entrepreneurship have failed to produce a relevant theory of economic growth, they have recognized the importance of change and have endeavored to elevate the entrepreneurial function to a more meaningful position. Space does not permit an exhaustive treatment of the literature on entrepreneurship, but a cursory review of the major thinkers and their contributions is in order.

Richard Cantillon in the late eighteenth century was the first to introduce the term entrepreneur into economic literature, defining it as the bearer of insurable risk.[2] Jean Baptiste Say in the early nineteenth century expanded the definition of the entrepreneurial function by stressing the interaction among the factors of production (land, labor, and capital) under conditions or risk. He clearly saw the entrepreneur as the prime agent directing resources from less productive to more productive results. At one point he noted that the entrepreneur is the person:

> who unites all the means of production—the labor of the one, the capital or the land of others—and who finds in the value of the products which result from their employment the reconciliation of the entire capital that he utilizes, and the value of wages, the interest, and the rent which he pays as well as the profits belonging to himself.[3]

Except in a peripheral way, the economic fraternity paid little attention to the original insight of Say. Although the entrepreneurial function was not seen as central to the economic process, a number of scholars recognized its significance in a tangential way. Robert Owen and Henri de St. Simon pointed out the managerial tasks of productivity and motivation. Karl Marx correctly saw that the productivity of capital resulted chiefly from the application of human abilities, but his insight into change was clouded by his penchant for proclaiming the class struggle as the chief force for economic change. Alfred Marshall saw the necessity to include management as a key factor or production along with land, labor and capital, but his inclination to focus on the small business firm as the representative unit meant that his treatment of entrepreneurship scarcely went beyond the recognition stage. Apparently, James H. Stauss was the first economist to note the shift of entrepreneurship as simply a function of proprietary ownership by advancing the proposition that "the firm is the entrepreneur."[4]

Students of the entrepreneurial process owe an enormous intellectual debt to the Harvard economist, Joseph Schumpeter, one of the most distinguished academic minds of the twentieth century. As early as 1911, in his pioneering work, *The Theory of Economic Development*, Schumpeter saw the function of innovation as the major source of economic change, mirroring itself by the following activities:

> This concept covers the following five cases: (1) The introduction of a new good—that is one which customers are not yet familiar—or a new quality or good. (2) The introduction of a new method of production, that is one not yet tested by experience in the branch of manufacture concerned, which need by no means be founded upon a discovery scientifically new, and can also exist in a new way of handling a product commercially. (3) The opening of a new market, that is a market into which the particular branch of manufacture of the country in question has not previously entered, whether or not this market has existed before. (4) The conquest of a new source of supply of raw materials or half-manufactured goods, again irrespective of whether this source already exists or whether it has first to be created. (5) The carrying out of new organizations in any industry like the creation of a monopoly position (for example through trustification) or the breaking up of a monopoly position.[5]

In elaborating on the concept of innovation almost a generation later in *Business Cycles*, Schumpeter's approach remains consistent; he stresses, however, that it should not be narrowly equated with invention.

> By changes in the methods of supplying commodities we mean a range of events much broader than the phrase covers in the literal acceptance. We include the introduction of new commodities which may even serve as the standard case. Technological change in the production of commodities already in use, the opening up of new markets or of new sources of supply, Taylorization of work, improved handling of material, the setting up of new business organizations such as department stores—in short, any "doing things differently" in the realm of economic life—all these are instances of what we shall refer to as the term Innovation. It should be noticed at once that the concept is not synonomous with "invention" (see Chap. I, Sect. B). Whatever the latter term may mean, it has but a distant relation to ours. Moreover, it carries misleading associations.[6]

In advancing the notions of innovation and "creative destruction," Schumpeter viewed the entrepreneur as the central figure of dynamic capitalism. At the same time Schumpeter never carried his insights to their ultimate conclusion in developing a systematic theory. In focusing on capitalism rather than management, Schumpeter stressed that economic equilibrium was related to the disturbances of the innovator. In reacting to the swings of the business cycle Schumpeter saw the innovator as a creative social agent who, if he reacted to environmental conditions successfully, paved the way for a new economic equilibrium. Apparently Schumpeter was less aware of the importance of innovation as a survival function within the typical business.

Schumpeter visualized the result of a major innovation as a singular and exceptional event, and after it was accomplished successfully by the entrepreneur, the economic system could look forward to a sustained period of continued equilibrium. Consequently, he viewed the typical businessman as engaging chiefly in operational activities; the innovator was the exception. In his concept of innovation Schumpeter did not indicate how the businessman undertook the task of adapting to changing conditions of the business cycle. Despite his notable contributions, he apparently did not see entrepreneurship as a purposeful activity capable of being systematically organized within the enterprise.

Moreover, Schumpeter was pessimistic about the long run prospects of entreprenurial activity in rescuing the capitalist system from its inherent vulnerabilities of depression, business cycle, inflation and unemployment. Although he recognized the futility of centralized planning as an alternative, Schumpeter was almost as dogmatic as any Marxist or socialist ideologue on the capabilities of capitalism renewing itself over the long haul. In his celebrated work, *Capitalism, Socialism and Democracy,* he foresaw even the exceptional businessman losing his energetic powers, those which in the past justified his existence by his contributing to the growth of capitalism and also preventing its collapse. According to Schumpeter, the erosion of the innovating spirit under conditions of mature capitalism was inevitable because of the decay of business purpose and incentives, its lack of defenses against governmental interference and hostility from intellectuals. Schumpeter may yet be proven right in his assessment of the cultural contradictions of capitalism, but businessmen have no alternative but to try to overcome his perceptive reservations about the system.[7]

With few exceptions in the recent past, most notably the British economist G.L.S. Shackle, most modern economists have ignored the entrepreneurial process. As William Baumol has pointed out, economists have continued the tradition of stressing optimality analysis of well-defined problems with the entrepreneur relegated to the position of a passive risk bearer.[8]

From a theoretical point of view, however, one optimistic sign appears on the academic horizon. In recent years the discipline of financial management has attempted to deal with the problems of corporate growth in both a more pragmatic and scholarly fashion. Although the challenge of formulating a general theory of entrepreneurship still remains elusive, such theorists as Joel Dean, Robert Anthony, Edith Penrose, Neil Chamberlain, and Ezra Solomon,[9] to cite a few, have added to our insights in the area of profit, cost analysis, deployment of resources, capital budgeting and financial leverage. Most important in seeing the enterprise as more than a tool kit of financial techniques, these financial management scholars, by focusing on the management of change and asset management in a more profound fashion, are headed in the right direction.

Economic History

In tracing company histories, economic historians have produced many excellent entrepreneurial case studies. The expectation, however, that an exploration into business history will provide profound insights into the entrepreneurial process encounters immediate disappointment. In mirroring descriptive activities of individual entrepreneurs, the focus is usually related to the men who started the business. Business histories are rich in descriptive detail, but provide no systematic pattern of corporate entrepreneurial activity. The stories tell little of decision making concerning risk and opportunity on the corporate level. The anecdotes of the business historians are informative and interesting, but it is difficult to imagine how the modern manager can discern relevant guidelines from these narrow cases of clinical success in implementing the practice of managing change.

Management Theory

Management theory, an infant among academic disciplines, had its origin around the turn of the century. Along with economists and historians, management scholars have not accorded a prominent place to the entrepreneurial function. They do not deny the entrepreneur's existence, but they usually relegate his role to the status of an irrational mystique, instead of a function capable of being systematically organized. Most of

Entrepreneurship

the management literature mentions the importance of entrepreneurship in the opening chapter, but the reader rarely, if ever, sees another mention except in the index.

The explanation for the entrepreneurial vacuum in management theory is not difficult to discern. Among the most prominent reasons for the neglect are: the excessive concern with quantifying the internal activities of the business during the past two generations, the techniques of measurement and validity taking precedence over the vision of risk and opportunity; the proclivity of managers to tolerate change but not encourage it, resulting frequently in the revolutionaries of yesterday becoming the staunchest defenders of the status quo; and, finally, the inability of most business professionals to recognize their specialized contributions as part of a larger business totality. In short, management literature dwells most heavily upon administration which has received disproportionate attention at the expense of entrepreneurship.

The Entrepreneurial Personality

Confining the entrepreneurial function into a routine catechism of rules and formulae is an impossible assignment. Entrepreneurs must make commitments under conditions of uncertainty. Risk taking judgment is neither conducive to proof nor disproof. All we can say for certain is that commitments to economic results must be relevant to the entrepreneurial tasks.

The human being is, however, at the center of the entrepreneurial decision making process. The corporation does not make decisions; people do. It is understandable why most economists exclude the human being from their models, since any discussion of human beings involves attitudes, behavior, motivation, personality, judgment, perception, and ability. No economist can handle adequately all the complex variables. Complexity notwithstanding, temperament is important and raises the issue of the entrepreneurial personality.

In the early nineteenth century, Jean Baptiste Say attempted a personality profile of the entrepreneur, and modern scholarship has not improved upon his definition to any notable degree. He set forth the following entrepreneurial characteristics:

> . . . judgment, perseverance, and a knowledge of the world as well as of the business. He is called upon to estimate with tolerable accuracy the importance of the specific product, the probable amount of demand and the means of production; at

the same time he must employ a great number of hands and give at all times a rigid attention to order and economy; in a word, he must possess the art of superintendence and administration. . . . In the course of such complex operations there are abundance of obstacles to be surmounted, of anxieties to be repressed, and of expedients to be desired.[10]

As Say noted, entrepreneurship calls for a temperament dealing with many subtle human activities. Ideally, it demands an artistic attitude which the individual must impose on himself. Among some of the broad traits associated with most entrepreneurial personalities are the following: an innovating point of view, tolerance toward uncertainty, willingness to assume accountability for risks, ability to undertake unpopular missions, a desire for achievement, perception of the importance of external business forces, a heavy quotient of self-confidence, analytical skill in diagnosing opportunities, conceptual skill in formulating alternative strategies, responsibility for managing change, and a focus on economic results rather than problems. However, just as no two chefs run their kitchens the same way, no two entrepreneurs will have identical personalities. Because entrepreneurship is a human volitional process dealing with a dynamic environment and an uncertain tomorrow it must always include a prominent place for artistry and imagination. Theory is always useful but it is not a substitute for art. When any art becomes popular it ceases to be an art; entrepreneurship is no exception. At the same time, although it is impossible to teach an art, it is possible to learn some of the skills on which the art rests. In establishing an atmosphere for systematic learning it is possible to raise the level of any discipline enabling mediocre practitioners to achieve superior performance.

The Role of Creativity

In improving the state of the entrepreneurial art, many businesses have placed great stock in creativity. The emphasis is misplaced and exaggerated; creativity is not crucial. In general, entrepreneurial creativity cannot be decreed by administrative fiat. Energy can only be released by establishing the proper atmosphere for business growth. Creativity without the appropriate vision of the business will result in irrelevance. Providing the specialist with more freedom, for example, will generally result in more specialization.

Most companies have more creative ideas than they are able to use effectively. The trouble with most creativity is that people fail to do anything about their insights. Unless ideas are translated into effective action, converted into priority commitments, and implemented into work assignments, the brilliant ideas will remain sterile. Creativity in isolation is inadequate; entrepreneurship means effective action for economic results. Creativity, moreover, places undue emphasis on the temperament of the individual entrepreneur. This approach has some validity for starting a new business, but for an ongoing business the organizing of the entrepreneurial function is the central task. In a mature business the team approach to entrepreneurship assumes an amalgam of many temperaments. In any effort to systematize the entrepreneurial function, creativity, or the formulation of new ideas *per se*, will probably be the least of the problems.

The Behavioral and Social Sciences

In recent years behavioral and social scientists have devoted considerable attention to the subject of entrepreneurship. David McClellan, Thomas Cochran, Everett Hagan, and Fritz Redlich[11] have, in one fashion or another, sought to identify the motivation inherent in the entrepreneurial personality. Their efforts are noble, but all lack empirical verification. In light of the complexity of the task it is important to recall Schumpeter's words: "Economic activity may have many motives, even a spiritual one, but its meaning is always the satisfaction of wants."[12] Instead of trying to obtain questionable dividends in discovering the personality traits of the entrepreneur, perhaps a sounder and more immediate approach is to recognize commitment to *the task* as essential. Again the words of Schumpeter are instructive: "Then there is a will to conquer: the impulse to fight, to prove oneself superior to others, to succeed for the sake, not the fruits of success but the success itself."[13]

Organizational Restraints

If the search for the entrepreneurial personality has more shadow than substance and if the quest for creativity as a panacea is an oversimplification, there is still another obstacle militating against entrepreneurship in almost all large organizations. For a number of reasons individuals with potential entrepreneurial attitudes find the sledding tough in large corporations. First, entrepreneurship is seen as a superfunction resting with one man or with a small group of men.

Second, the function is further obscured by specialized and operational work. The specialist focuses on rules, procedures, internal needs, administrative work, costs, the past and stability. The entrepreneur. on the other hand, emphasizes change, the environment, economic results and future opportunities. The specialist and the entrepreneur are both important, but each does different things. Each has different criteria of performance and each works in different time spans. Contrary to being innovative minded, the premium for the administrator performing routine operating tasks is on not being conspicuous. The reward system focuses on operations which means keeping a low profile. Entrepreneurial versatility demands a different style from administrative ability. Operational work will require continued competency, but it must be supplemented with entrepreneurial activity, the combination of entrepreneurial and specialized functions in a single person is, of course, both feasible and desirable, but it will always be the ability to assume risks and maximize opportunities that separate the entrepreneur from the average manager.

The reality of the business as an information system is that all functions and levels are concerned with entrepreneurship. The cost accountant in defining terms, the research man in producing new products, the marketing specialist in focusing on the customer, the quality control engineer in his listing of specifications, the personnel man in his selection of people—all are involved in implementing the entrepreneurial function. The problem is that each of these specialists has trouble obtaining feedback in terms of the outside environment and economic results. From a strictly entrepreneurial point of view there is no such thing as a functional decision (financial, marketing, production, etc.); there is only a business or management decision. All of which suggests the need to enlarge the concept of the entrepreneur beyond top management.

Finally, the larger the organization the more difficult it is to tackle the entrepreneurial task. One of the advantages of a large corporation is that its resources allow it more staying power. At the same time this quality permits entrenched bureaucracies to pay less attention to the entrepreneurial function. Change upsets the bureaucrat, disrupting his pattern of certainty and consistency. The larger the organization the greater the tendency to concentrate on the inside (communication, procedures, paper work, problems, etc.) at the expense of external opportunities and results for the business as a whole.

The efforts of behavioral and social scientists in identifying entrepreneurial personalities have not produced rich dividends. Most of the research has been descriptive; and developing a person with all the necessary traits is tantamount to searching for the unicorn. The major difficulty is that we want individuals who are functionally specialized in one area, but who also have the managerial literacy to understand the many sub-disciplines of the enterprise. At the same time, we want them to manage change. The challenge is demanding and obviously not all can qualify. Perhaps we should recognize that in endeavoring to develop an entrepreneurial mentality, we are attempting to accomplish the highly improbable. At the same time we have no choice but to try to meet the challenge or else admit the impossibility of systematizing economic performance. The starting point for the entrepreneurial task is a more sophisticated understanding of the concepts of uncertainty and profit and a deeper analysis of risk and opportunity, because they are the important vehicles for achieving economic results.

THE CONCEPTS OF UNCERTAINTY, PROFIT, RISK AND OPPORTUNITY

Uncertainty

According to the premises of classical economics perfect knowledge or certainty was assumed, but uncertainty, the gap between what is known and what needs to be known, is the prevailing norm of the entrepreneurial process. Whereas risk generally refers to the probabilistic cost outcomes of alternative actions, uncertainty is more subjective, encompassing within it the degree of confidence in the entrepreneur's expectations for economic results. But even more critical are the uncertainties of the external realm whose variables are incapable of control and rarely subject to exact quantitative treatment. Precision prevails only in the illusory non-existent state of economic models. In the real world all managers making commitments are destined to have a rendezvous with uncertainty. The problem for the entrepreneur is to narrow the gap between uncertainty and knowledge by seeking a methodology for reducing uncertainty. The challenge is a major one which has received only limited attention within the mainstream of economics over the past two generations. Two economists who have attacked this problem, however, are Frank Knight[14] and G.L.S. Shackle.[15]

Over fifty years ago, Frank Knight, of the University of Chicago, pioneered the approach toward a methodology when he contended that the most feasible strategy in dealing with uncertainty was the acquisition of improved business knowledge. In associating the search for knowledge with the pursuit of profit to reduce economic uncertainty, Knight visualized knowledge as the nourishment input creating profit, the food of economic survival. Improved knowledge enabled the business organism to enlarge its purpose and undertake future economic actions. He also added another dimension to the entrepreneurial task when he pointed out that insurable risks amount to another form of business costs and that economic profits result from successfully dealing with uncertainty or a non-measurable risk. Knight notes that the uncertainty of the unique event is the key to profit when he states:

> The only risk which leads to a profit is a unique uncertainty resulting from an exercise of ultimate responsibility which in its very nature cannot be insured, nor capitalized nor salaried. Profit arises out of the absolute unpredictability of things, out of the sheer brute fact that the results of human activity cannot be anticipated and then only in so far as even a profitability calculus in regard to them is impossible and meaningless.[16]

According to Knight, the assumption of perfect knowledge in classical economic doctrine exalted the role of the administrator and eliminated the need for the entrepreneur. He maintained that uncertainty is actually the source of business change.

> With uncertainty absent man's energies are devoted altogether to today's things; it is doubtful whether intelligence itself would exist in such a situation; in a world so built that perfect knowledge was theoretically possible, it seems likely .hat all organic adjustments would become mechanical. With uncertainty present, doing things the actual execution of activity, becomes in a real sense a secondary part of life; the primary problem or function is deciding what to do and how to do it.[17]

Shackle endorses Knight's criticism of probability based on frequency distribution in traditional economic doctrine and stresses the importance of the unique event in entrepreneurial decision making. He admits that complete certainty is impossible, but contends that improved and systematic knowledge will assist the manager in his quest for greater certainty. He argues, furthermore, a deeper understanding of short and long term business outcomes, along with recognizing the distinction between controllable and non-controllable events will provide management with a sounder approach for reducing uncertainty. Shackle proposes that the manager deemphasize probability which too often tends to treat dynamic problems from static assumptions and substitute a more qualitative methodology to business decision making pivoting around two main themes: (1) the relative gain or loss connected with various business choices; and (2) the degree of strength and weaknesses involved in entrepreneurial expectations.

On the first point, Shackle suggests that the economic decision maker should choose between two sets of alternatives, "focus gain" (the economic results he anticipates) and "focus loss" (the degree of uncertainty he associates with the outcome). In discussing the second point of expectation, Shackle introduces the highly original idea of "potential surprise" into economic literature, when he states:

> A man cannot, in general, tell what will happen, but his conception of the nature of things, the nature of men and their institutions and affairs and of the non-human world, enable him to form a judgment as to whether any suggested thing can happen. In telling himself that such a thing "can" happen, he means that its occurrence would not "surprise" him; for we are surprised by the occurrence of what we had supposed to be against nature. . . . If a man feels that, should his knowledge and understanding remain as they are, the occurrence of a given thing would not surprise him in the slightest degree, we may say that for him, that thing is "perfectly possible." We are "taking certainty of the wrongness" of a proposition to be a state of mind familiar to everyone and needing no definition.[18]

Shackle considers "potential surprise" as ranging from the extremes of almost perfect plausibility to absolute disbelief. He elaborates:

> Zero potential surprise attached to a hypothesis means that this hypothesis is looked on as "perfectly possible," as perfectly consistent with the individual's existing knowledge. The number of distinct answers to some one question, to which a person can simultaneously assign zero potential surprise, is unlimited. Because certainty of the truth implies that all rival hypotheses are completely excluded, it implies that these rivals are assigned the absolute maximum of potential surprise. Thus potential surprise, though representing disbelief, is something quite other than the mere inverse of the degree of positive belief or confidence; for if it were such an inverse, subjective perfect certainty of the truth of a hypothesis could be represented by merely assigning it to zero potential surprise.[19]

Shackle equates the entrepreneurial pursuit of profit with the pursuit of knowledge. He puts it in the following pragmatic fashion:

> To forget that the business of living, and within that larger whole, the business of producing and exchanging goods, essentially and inescapably involves and requires the continuous and endless gaining of knowledge, is to divorce our theories from half their subject matter. To say that there is always potential for new knowledge to be gained is to say that possessed knowledge is always incomplete, unsure and potentially wrong . . . . All is experiment.[20]

He concludes that the more successful the entrepreneur is in fulfilling customer wants, the more he reduces uncertainty. His approach is somewhat akin to the modern marketing concept which has been largely neglected by economic theorists. At the present time more empirical evidence is needed to support Shackle's theory of decision making, this will not be easy, however, because of the complexity of the subject. Nevertheless, his approach is refreshing if only because he argues that entrepreneurial questions should precede any concern with economic techniques and tools. More specifically his position raises questions about the computer and its role in improving business knowledge.

Business practitioners placed high hopes on the computer as the key business tool in eliminating uncertainty. However, as Shackle suggests, the entrepreneurial problem centers more on risk taking judgment under conditions of uncertainty than inert information. The computer cannot convert information into judgments. It is impossible to quantify what we cannot define or to solve equations consisting only of unknowns. The computer is a remarkable tool capable of calculations at incredible speeds. However, as a method of reducing uncertainty its results have been disappointing, largely because it has been used as a fountainhead of answers rather than a source of proper questions. Ideally, the great promise and power of the computer rests in its capacity as a question asking machine in the search for improved knowledge in selecting alternatives. In sacrificing relevance for validity, it has been a misused tool. Instead of providing solutions the computer should be used to get entrepreneurial alternatives. If the manager is presented with a range of alternative options by the management scientist, he will be in a better position to reduce uncertainty by focusing on the relevant risks and selecting the best opportunities.

PROFIT MYOPIA

The disciplines of accounting and economics are indispensable informational centers of business practice. But as with the computer, their applications to entrepreneurship have been fragmented and of limited relevance. Accountants perceive the business from the angle of the past, viewing profits from the point of view of overhead and liquidation rather than as utility and as a wealth producing instrument. Except in those instances of treating accelerated depreciation and resource preservation in dealing with inflation, the accounting focus is primarily on cost, neglecting risk, opportunity and the capital needs of the future. Accountants measure economic results in a variety of ways (return on investment, return on sales, cash flow, etc.), often confirming the criticism that despite excessive quantification the results are more metaphysical than precise. Because of the difficult problem in deciding what costs are relevant and quantifiable, profit measurement assumes many shapes and forms. Efforts to achieve precision in the accountant's ledger obscures the qualitative feature of profitability.

Economic theory also deals with growth problems but within the framework of static assumptions. The result is atomization which fails to visualize the economic components interacting in the total business process. Instead of seeing profit in the total spectrum of the firm's growth, economic theory views it as a marginal economic function, measuring the cost allocation of land, labor and capital. From an entrepreneurial point of view, an understanding of profit calls for a shift from cost to risk and opportunity.

Three prominent scholars, Oskar Morgenstern, Ezra Solomon, and Peter Drucker, take serious issue with the methods used by accountants and economists in depicting the role of profit in the business enterprise.[21] Some of their comments on how the conventional models distort the reality of the profit picture are worth noting.

According to Morgenstern, balance sheet figures, while not entirely meaningless, tell little about authentic economic results. He argues that profit and loss statements, determination of costs, payment of dividends, etc., do not contain the precision and objectivity implied in them. They result from decisions which antedate the bottom line of alleged performance. Company tradition, the behavior of other firms, expectations, prestige, etc., all display subjective bias in determining how much to pay out in dividends and how much to retain as surplus. Morgenstern states: "The idea that profits are the automatic consequence of costs of production and sales, on the one hand, and receipts from sales on the other, is naive and has nothing to do with business reality. Economic reality does not deal with the real world and it does not take into account these practices."[22]

Ezra Solomon is also highly critical of the specious accuracy of the profit picture, particularly when it is viewed solely as an owner-oriented concept, i.e., providing returns for those who render the equity capital to the business. This conventional wisdom, according to Solomon, is a poor guide to business action since it focuses on profit maximization and not wealth maximization, the latter being the true mission of the business.[23]

For the past thirty years in his numerous books and articles, Peter Drucker has been even more critical of the traditional interpretation of profit.[24] He argues recently that there is no such thing as profit, there are only costs. He cites the three main costs for any business as: the cost of current business activity, the uncertainty of future business activity, and the costs of jobs and pensions for tomorrow. If a business only meets the first one and neglects the other two, it is actually operating at a loss, regardless of what the balance sheet claims. Although the three costs overlap they are as much a part of the economic reality for the firm's survival as payment of wages, dividends and supplies. Unless business management assumes the responsibility for future costs as well as present costs, profit is a delusion. For Drucker, the key question is not profit maximization but "What is the minimum profitability needed to cover the future needs of the business?"[25]

Profit and Profitability

The profit maximization concept of the traditional accounting and economic models is a limited operational guideline in modern corporate decision making. It is seriously deficient and clouds the entrepreneurial function for the following interrelated reasons: (1) stress on owner-orientation, (2) restricted scope of activity, (3) limited time horizon, (4) neglect of future costs and expected benefits, (5) creation of social hostility, and (6) misplaced emphasis on the profit motive. A few brief words on each are in order.

Stress on Owner-Orientation

The underlying idea of profit in classical economics is a deceptively simple one. In an engineering and physical science sense it is the ratio between inputs or efforts and outputs or results, with the latter flowing into the hands of the owners. The notion of profit maximization is a legacy of an earlier era of business structure based on the authority of private property. In the economic model of Adam Smith, owners of the business enterprise were expected to pursue individual self-interest, which when combined with competition and the "invisible hand" of the marketplace resulted automatically in progress and wealth for society.

Around the turn of the century a new corporate structure emerged, characterized chiefly by the separation of ownership and control and the rise of a professional managerial class. Ideology, however, failed to keep abreast of business reality. As an operating business guideline profit maximization, according to Robert Anthony, became increasingly unrealistic, misleading and immoral.[26]

Because profit maximization is an owner-oriented concept, it focuses on the amount and share of corporate income which goes to those providing the equity capital of the business. Viewing the corporation from the single legal dimension of rewarding the private property of shareholders, it is concerned primarily with the amount of corporate wealth going to the owners. The modern corporation, however, has more than just the shareholder claims to consider in distributing income; it also has a responsibility in meeting the claims of employees, management, future costs and society. Management must continue to provide stockholders with a fair and satisfactory return of profits, but it must be done within a system of tradeoffs among other claimants.

Restricted Scope of Business Activity

Profit maximization is an inadequate guide for business planning because it restricts itself to the one dominant objective of finance. Many businesses currently mirroring outstanding "bottom line" performance are readily identifiable. At the same time it is quite probable that many of them will not be in business three to five years hence. Their corporate profit picture shows only the top of the business iceberg. In concentrating exclusively on the financial yardstick, these businesses are neglecting other survival objectives such as: innovation, marketing, the human organization and the environment. All of these critical business activities involve uncertainty; and, hence, do not appear in the ledger. But they are real costs and continued neglect of them today could threaten the survival of the business tomorrow.

The management career of Sewall Avery, the former head of Montgomery Ward, is instructive, because he was probably the last major leader who followed literally the principle of profit maximization.

In the years following World War II, the net earnings of Montgomery Ward were higher than its chief competitor, Sears Roebuck. Acting on the assumption of an approaching depression, Avery hoarded his reserves; whereas Sears, foreseeing an environment of growth for American society, was investing its capital in new opportunities. Avery's fallacy was to equate the future exclusively in a narrow monetary fashion and rewarding owners in the immediate short run.

Limited Time Horizon

Measuring profit for a one-year period is misleading because it sees the business from the viewpoint of liquidation, that is, what it can be sold for at the present time. The limited time span neglects to take into account future alternative courses of action for maximizing business wealth. The rate of profit per annum describes past relationships of expenditure of effort compared to results, but ignores future commitments and benefits.

Neglect of Future Costs and Benefits

Maximization of profits is of no assistance in performing the entrepreneurial task because it fails to take uncertainty into account. In an unknowable future world neither the quantity nor the rate of profit is a useful tool in factoring in future costs and expected benefits. It tells nothing about allocating for risk proper; the cost of staying in business; the source of capital for opportunities and business growth; and the source of capital to finance new jobs. All these areas involve uncertainty and hence do not appear in the ledger. These real costs, if continually disregarded could threaten the survival of any business.

Creation of Public Hostility

If the myopia of profit maximization was confined strictly to academe, the impact would be insignificant. But the faulty vision has found its way into the behavior of many business managements. Ask a typical business audience the chief purpose of any business and the overwhelming response will be to make money. Viewing the business as the exclusive pursuit of profit is not only irrelevant, it misdirects business activities and allows society to misinterpret the real mission of business. It creates hostility from the outside by creating the false impression that business is exploiting the public by its unjust profits. In a

Entrepreneurship

recent poll the public believed that business earned thirty-three percent return on sales; the figure is closer to five percent with inflation factored in. Consequently, it is hardly surprising that the populists, desiring short term income redistribution, demand the curbing of profits to a one or two percent level instead of the percentage necessary to maintain a healthy economic growth for society.

Misplaced Emphasis on the Profit Motive

Much of the misconception on the role of profits stems from the stress of economic theory on economic man with the accompanying profit motive. Instead of attempting to address itself to the function of entrepreneurship, classical economics emphasizes the pecuniary motivation of man. The result is both poor economics and distorted history. Although many have attempted to point out the irrelevancy of the profit motive, the view persists.

The idea of profit motive, moreover, infers cause or purpose whereas profit is actually a result of business performance. Whether the individual businessman is personally motivated by profit is a matter of private concern between him and his conscience. If he feels a compulsion to make a report to confess his personal contribution to the Gross National Product, it is a private matter which fails to illuminate his entrepreneurial activities as a businessman. The profit motive may have limited relevance for the owner-entrepreneur who starts his business, but even this is debatable. In this case the business is a personal extension of himself. But once a company transcends the life of a single individual, the business becomes organized for perpetuity and has survival imperatives of its own.

Profitability

Considering the aforementioned limitations of profit maximization in conforming to modern corporate reality, it is difficult to see any management considering it as an operational guideline for financial planning. Profitability is a far more relevant term because it focuses on the maximizing of wealth or present net worth. According to Ezra Solomon, wealth or net present worth is "the difference between gross present worth and the amount of capital investment required to achieve the benefits being discussed."[27] The definition of wealth maximization helps provide a perspective for the more profound meaning of profitability including such functions as: a measurement and feedback for economic performance, a condition of survival, the costs of staying in business, the role of future costs and the risk and uncertainty factors connected with maximizing opportunities.

Profitability, then, is an essential condition, but it must share its place with other survival requirements (marketing, social responsibility, innovation, human organization, etc.) of the enterprise. When profit is seen as one of the many interdependent survival conditions, its critical role in the entrepreneurial process becomes sharper. Assuming risk and opportunity to obtain expansion, we must also assume uncertainty. Profitability, in effect, becomes the cost of uncertainty. Although tomorrow's commitments can only be measured imprecisely within a rough range of probability, their costs are as real as past costs. The manager will continue to ask the question with respect to past costs if there is enough revenue to cover them; but, he must with respect to the uncertain future also ask whether there is sufficient revenue to meet tomorrow's commitments. Whether this future need is called profit, profitability, economic surplus, capital or socialist accumulation is less important than understanding the real significance of the concept.

At the same time, in order to present an improved picture of profit to the public, the semantical aspect deserves far more attention than it has previously received from American businessmen. Unfortunately, as the opinion polls previously cited attest, the popular image conveys an image of exploitation and unjust reward. Reginald Jones, Chairman of General Electric, suggests businessmen stop using the term regardless of its revered accounting tradition. He proposes that it would be more relevant to separate the present definition of profit into three categories: first, taxes which siphon off almost half; second, the portion paid out to stockholders in the form of dividends (which Jones maintains is actually the use of people's savings, representing interest paid on loans); third, the remainder allocated to reinvestment (which according to Jones should be labeled business savings or reinvested earnings). In short, Jones concludes that the categories of taxes, interest on earnings, and savings are familiar terms in the family budget. The use of these terms has advantages over the generic use of profit and would help eliminate some of its pejorative connotations. Whether it is possible to translate Jones' approach into reality is another question. But one thing is certain, his candid critique is a frank admission that businessmen have failed to explain the true mission of profits to the American people.[28]

Profitability is a survival responsibility of any economic system.

The Soviet Union's socialist economic model, for example, requires greater profitability or socialist accumulation because it has no instrument allowing for abandonment of non-productive enterprises. Moreover, instead of allowing the market to be the major allocator of resources, the Soviet model is saddled with oppressive bureaucratic price and wage controls, a centralized pattern of industrial risk taking and a wasteful cost structure which, in order to sustain the system further, adds to the need of greater profitability. In the American system the function of loss or the ability not to make a profit is crucial to the system. The factoring in of failure assures abandonment so that in the long run growth can be achieved by getting the revenues of profitability into the appropriate risks and relevant opportunities. Rather than serving a narrow economic function of being a reward for capital, labor and land costs, profitability is the reward for risk taking. At the same time, however, because the market system has the inherent risk of loss and the feature of constant uncertainty, management will always face the ceaseless challenge of performing an encore of economic performance.

RISK AND OPPORTUNITY

Boehm-Bawork's Theorem

Eugene Boehm-Bawork, the noted Austrian economist, introduced a provocative entrepreneurial theorem which states that existing means of production will yield greater economic performance only through increased uncertainty, that is, through greater risk.[29]

A central core of Boehm-Bawork's analysis is the concept of "roundabout production," e.g., the generation of current economic assets from past business achievements. Essentially, it is an argument for superior productive benefits accruing from more elaborate technology as opposed to primitive technology. The more sophisticated technology, however, will cost more and require a greater infusion of risk capital. In most instances, without facing up to the risk and uncertainty factors of improving technology or "roundabout production," there is usually no other way of satisfying consumer needs.[30] Boehm-Bawork saw the value of capital as a productive risk taking instrument ". . . because it finds its destination in the production of goods; further because it is an effectual tool in completing the roundabout and profitable methods of production once they are entered upon; finally because it makes the adoption of new and profitable methods possible."[31]

Boehm-Bawork placed special emphasis on the significance of the time factor in business decision making. He argued that past economic achievements act as a restraining influence on new commitments. The favoring of the past over the future arises from the businessmen's greater familiarity with prior accomplishments when compared with the unknowable future. In placing a higher subjective value on the present and discounting the future, the normal tendency of the businessman is to minimize risk because of the optimistic belief that the future will somehow or other take care of itself. As a result the nonentrepreneurial businessman will tend to overstate present means, while assigning a low priority to the future benefits of the business. If the businessman favors present technology for an indefinite period of time, he faces additional risk because of the greater stress and increased rigidity associated with operating current plant and equipment. The danger of business survival becomes more pronounced as the amount of generated assets or "roundabout production" within the firm increases. The greater the economic stakes, the greater the risk.

Boehm-Bawork's theorem is an excellent platform for launching an understanding of the complex interrelationship between risk and opportunity. Inherent in his theorem are such inferences as the qualitative difference between undertaking risks in a new business venture versus the risks in an ongoing business operation, the need to view entrepreneurship as a process, and an insight into the ambiguities of the term risk.

A New Business Versus Ongoing Business Risks

The qualitative distinction in terms of risk and opportunity between the entrepreneur starting the business and the entrepreneurial function operating within an ongoing business organized for perpetuity is inferred in Boehm-Bawork's theorem. The distinction between the individual and the corporate function may be clearer in contrasting the entrepreneurial decisions of Henry Ford I and Henry Ford II. The elder Ford may have taken great personal risks in terms of his limited wealth when he originally invested $28,000 to start the Ford Motor Company. Henry Ford II, a generation later with a much larger economic infrastructure, undertook a much greater corporate risk when he budgeted approximately a half billion dollars to bring the Edsel on the market. The Edsel failed, raising the question how many such marketing fiascoes a company as large

Entrepreneurship

as Ford could tolerate. The answer hinges on many factors, depending on how the subjective nature of the risk is defined. However, in huge corporations with massive assets there is a greater increase of risk taking as assets are enlarged. In many instances, it is not unusual for managers to bet their company's future when they undertake major strategic economic decisions.

Entrepreneurship as a Process

The theorem recognizes the need to view entrepreneurship as a process composed of present and future time phases in treating the components of risk and opportunity. Economic performance dictates that risk must be faced because there can be no new economic achievement without change and no change without risk. It also implies the need for systematic and improved performance of the ongoing business in order to assure greater resources for taking risks. Everything a business does includes risk and the farther ahead it plans the greater the risk factor. Because risk cannot be avoided, especially in periods of rapid change, it must be courted rather than feared. Indeed, superior economic performance can be defined as the ability to take greater risks. Any business trying to escape risk will end up with the greatest risk of all—the risk of doing nothing. At the same time, in an economy of accelerating change a harsh new reality has emerged. On the one hand management must operate on the assumption of a lengthening time span before any economic results are realized. On the other, it is also probable that drastic changes in the environment will undermine the rationale of the original entrepreneurial decision.

Ambiguity of Risk

The term risk has many inherent ambiguities. In its actuarial sense it signifies a chance of loss as a knowable parameter of frequency distribution. In tossing a coin nobody can predict on any given call whether the outcome will be heads or tails. We know, however, that in an experiment of tossing the coin 24,000 times, the aggregate result will give us a fifty-fifty chance for either heads or tails.

Charles O. Hardy in his work, *Risk and Risk Bearing*, suggests the distinction between an actuarial or knowable risk and an entrepreneurial or unknowable risk when he states, "In a sense, all risks are due to ignorance for if all the conditions of any situation were known, there would be no risk involved in it for anyone. There is, however, a distinction worth maintaining between risks due to the limitations of human knowledge and risks which are due to the failure or inability of individuals to take advantage of the knowledge which is accessible to themselves."[33]

In the universe of entrepreneurial decision making, the focus is never on actuarial risk or statistical distribution in a series, but on the unique event. In pursuing the illusory path of quantitative assurance, we find a tendency to equate risk with certainty. At the same time, a measurable risk which of a more or less orderly nature is never the same as uncertainty, a condition always synonymous with ambiguity and disorder. An uninsurable risk is always characterized by uncertainty, and, in consequence, statistical assessment and probability are of little assistance. Classical economic theory, assuming perfect knowledge, views decision making under uncertainty as exceptional, but in entrepreneurial practice, the unknowable and the uncertain are the norms. Entrepreneurial decisions are never right or wrong in an arithmetical sense. The only form of quantification possible in risk taking is the degree that alternative options are "more or less" relevant. Admittedly the quantification of "more or less" is imprecise, but it is qualitatively real.

RISK AND OPPORTUNITY CHARACTERISTICS

In coming to grips with the interrelationships of uninsurable risk and opportunity, a few general assumptions are in order. First, the big opportunity without a large risk should be distrusted. If the opportunity is a major one, then the risk of money, people, effort and time must of necessity also be significant. High quantitative objectives automatically impose high qualitative objectives. The quixotic quest for a free lunch is even more inappropriate in entrepreneurship than it is in the rest of life.

Second, risk is a restraint; it is a preparation for action whereas opportunity is a ground for action. Just as the x-ray provides the doctor with a picture for patient diagnosis, risk analysis allows the manager to balance strategic tradeoffs, to factor in the element of timing, to assess resources and expectations, to determine the ratio between effort and potential impact, and to evaluate alternatives. All these risk factors mold the judgment toward opportunity—the avenue of anticipated action for economic results.

Third, the entrepreneur starts with risk because its parameters are definable. Yet, concentrating on "focus loss," or risk alone, is an invitation to inertia. The longer he dwells on risk, the greater the tendency to see only the red ink costs at the expense of results. Continued focus on risk is an invitation for everybody to raise objections and paralyze action. One thinks through risk slowly and carefully, but one acts swiftly on opportunity.

Fourth, the entrepreneurial approach assumes that companies should be opportunity oriented rather than problem focused. Concentrating on problems will invariably reflect the sparks of friction more than the glow of profits. Worrying about problems and disregarding opportunities is a certain sign that a company has passed its peak and is going downhill. Efficiency, doing a thing correctly, always becomes a secondary consideration compared to effectiveness or doing the right thing, which is what opportunity is all about. Operating work is still very important, but when a company is addressing itself to the proper entrepreneurial opportunity, it is usually too busy achieving economic results to worry disproportionately about internal problems. The most talented business brains in the country would achieve little if they were working on buggy whips, trolley cars, vacuum tubes and countless other economic fossils. Theodore Levitt, of Harvard University, put it crisply when he said, "In truth, I believe there is no such thing as a growth industry. There are only companies organized and operated to create and capitalize on growth opportunities."[34] All the great entrepreneurial success stories document this emphasis on opportunity. The lost opportunity never finds its way into the company balance sheet, but the missed opportunity often appears later in a plague of problems. The case studies of mismanagement verify this failure of entrepreneurial vision and action in neglecting opportunities.

Many managements smother opportunity by identifying goals that are impossible to translate into practice. For example, they stipulate that a new project fulfill the following paralyzing demands: a certain growth of so many million dollars in five years, association of the new product with the current line, a miserly budget for the project and a definite guaranteed profit margin of so much. Projects which do not conform to these mechanistic corporate policies are not considered worthy of financial support. In actuality, it is usually impossible for a new idea to pass through such a restricted screening process. In effect, such an unimaginative approach results in a pattern of circular stagnation in evaluating risk and opportunity. The approach is tantamount to saying no innovation is possible until the time is ripe for it—and the time is never ripe for it.

Finally, the probability is that major mistakes and losses will be encountered in assessing the interrelationship between risk and opportunity. With seven out of ten products failing, the successes must compensate for the unsuccessful dry hole ventures. Based on the assessment of risk and opportunity the real entrepreneurial decision is on commitment or "what do I stand for and believe in" when allocating resources.

CATEGORIES OF RISK AND OPPORTUNITY

No criteria of quantitative relevance exists in making an entrepreneurial decision on risk and opportunity. At best we can classify the interaction of the two components with regard to the means available for risk and the feasibility of opportunity.[35] Determining the extent to which risks are affordable and opportunities are attractive depends on the value judgment of management in estimating the degrees of uncertainty and the penalties for error.

First, there is the low level risk that any business can afford to take. Within this spectrum there is the guaranteed rate of return in a regulated industry or a patent right, which is really no risk at all, assuming an assured market is present. For most businesses the typical type of affordable risk is one that if the project fails the company will be economically injured, but not mortally wounded. Within this framework of a mildly affordable risk there is only the accompaniment of additive opportunity, that is, one which produces incremental economic results through either minor improvement in technology or an addition to the product line. The affordable risk is one in which the penalty for error will result in a short term loss of profit; and, if the venture succeeds, it will produce additional revenue but the basic mission of the business will remain the same. In short, appraisal of the affordable risk and additive opportunity, even a successful outcome will not alter the knowledge core or customer orientation of the business. For example, there are probably an endless variety of "new" cookies and crackers that could be introduced by Nabisco without substantially endangering the company's earnings or altering the future strategy of the business. The nature of business risk is probably the same for Gilette and the variety of blades it produces.

Second, there is the risk a business cannot afford to take. Paradoxically, this is the type of risk whereby a potential entrepreneurial success will not usually result in economic benefits. For example, in the case of a successful product in which the company does not have adequate dis-

Entrepreneurship

tribution ability or technical knowledge, the outcome will usually result in building up the business for somebody else. For products which do not fit into the knowledge and marketing strengths of the company, it may be more prudent to license or sell the product outright than undertake a commitment where there is no business competency. In those cases where competency is non-existent but the project is highly valued by management, the merger route may also be a plausible alternative. However, if management decides to stay with the project, there must be an awareness that it will virtually have to conduct a new business from conception, requiring a heavy commitment of time, people and capital.

Closely allied with the type of risk outside traditional business competency is the complementary opportunity. Typically, the complementary opportunity has a kinship to the central idea of the business, yet it is deceptive in that it is qualitatively different. When the oil companies entered the petro-chemical field, most were surprised to discover that petro-chemicals required radically different technological and marketing knowledge which had to be grafted on to the old oil business. In complementing the oil business with chemicals, the basic mission of the business was substantially changed. The same situation was encountered by lumber and steel companies in expanding their product line. They were forced to develop new knowledge and marketing competencies which subtly changed the purpose of their businesses.

Third, there is the risk that a business cannot afford not to take. This is the type of risk focusing on a potentially new and different business. If successful, it could wipe out the foundation of the old business. For example, if General Electric and Westinghouse failed to commit themselves to new forms of atomic and solar energy, then there probably might not be a business left when these new energy forms appeared on the economic scene. The opportunity side of this risk category is the genuine breakthrough, a major innovation changing the business beyond recognition and usually creating a whole new industry. Xerography, the computer and the transistor are classic examples in recent years. In those instances in which management foresees corporate death if there is no commitment to the opportunity, management must expect a new corporate mutation which will totally undermine the marketing premises and knowledge foundation of the old business.

The foregoing analysis of risk and opportunity does not contain answers for coping with the management of change; uncertainty precludes that. A risk and opportunity analysis, however, has the benefit of increasing management's sensitivity to a rapidly changing environment, assists in appraising tradeoffs of corporate resources, and strengthens the sense of total management entrepreneurial commitment throughout the organization.

In summary, the purpose of this chapter has not been to provide an in-depth analysis of entrepreneurial theory, but to point out the elusiveness of the term, the ambiguities of risk and uncertainty, and the various interpretations of profits. In addition, I have tried to highlight some of the major theoretical insights and contributions for students of management and operating managers.

As mentioned before, entrepreneurship has been a neglected topic in economic thought. In Leonard Silk's recent study of the five leading American economists (Paul Samuelson, Milton Friedman, John Galbraith, Wassily Leontief and Kenneth Boulding), the term is casually mentioned only four times.[36] But even among those thinkers who have identified the significance of entrepreneurship, there is missing a probing of entrepreneurial activity and the means of implementation. The following chapters will be addressed to that task of managing change more systematically by focusing on risk taking opportunities and shifting resources from less productive to more productive results.

CHAPTER III

Approaches to Entrepreneurial Strategies

All businesses performing successfully are in a state of dynamic equilibrium which, if undisturbed, have a tendency for energy to diffuse, success to become obsolete, effective performance to become marginal and for bureaucratic inertia to predominate. Charles Dailey warns us that because change won't manage itself automatically, the manager must manage change or else it will manage him.[1] Entrepreneurial direction is needed to counteract these tendencies of entropy and disintegration, the course of normal destiny for any enterprise following goals no longer relevant.

Failure to manage change means that the corporation will be overwhelmed by change. Edmund Burke once remarked that: "the state without some means of change is without the means of conservation."[2] Burke's words apply with equal cogency to the modern corporation. In a philosophical sense, the management of change is rapidly becoming the source of corporate legitimacy, superseding the old Lockean concept of ownership and property. Modern management is the leadership organ of society and its entrepreneurial task is to avoid decay by counteracting and reversing the potentially mindless drift of business as usual. The business corporation of today is not the final word. During its long history the corporation has undergone many mutations in adapting to changing environments. In tracing the historical origins of the corporation, it is possible to identify five major predominant forms of mutation: (1) medieval, (2) mercantilistic, (3) market, (4) managerial, and (5) multinational. In the midst of uncertainty and accelerating change, new strategic responses are required from the corporation which will result in a new mutational form. The most significant dimension of change shaping institutional corporate structure over the last generation has been the knowledge revolution. For example, approximately forty percent of the Gross National Product, and growing annually, is the production, consumption and dissemination of knowledge and information.[3] Perhaps the label "mental corporation" captures the emerging spirit of tomorrow's businesses.

The success of any individual business is the first early warning signal that it must modify its behavior, endeavor to avoid potential surprise and undertake a more systematic deployment of its resources. The drift of many firms into marginality, mediocrity and decline is largely attributable to a corporation's inability to manage change in an organized way. Even the giants of business are not exempt from extinction if they fail to pay attention to changes in the environment. Of the one hundred leading manufacturing firms of 1917, twenty-eight have gone out of business and fifty-four have been pushed off the top one hundred list.[4] One has only to think of Packard cars, Underwood typewriters, Atwater Kent radios and Eskimo Pies, among a host of others which were once revered brands but are no longer available.

The vision of entrepreneurial opportunities, however, alone provides no assurance of success; indeed a heavy probability of failure is always present. General Electric, RCA and Westinghouse, for example, all with competent managements, lost out in the computer market. Although these companies failed in this instance, they have also had other notable successes. The important point is that they had the advantage of choosing their commitments instead of having them thrust upon them by inertia. In short, the effort of systematically managing change is no guarantee of performance, but as many entrepreneurial success stories indicate, it is superior to drift. This is particularly true when one recognizes the importance of the principle that success always renders obsolete past realities.

Given the absence of meaningful theories of business growth, the manager must depend on intelligent actions in charting the course of change. The first step in formulating entrepreneurial strategies is recognizing the limitations of today's stable state and simultaneously recognize the awareness that tomorrow will be different. Understanding the past remains important, but mainly with regard to how certain decisions have transported us to where we are today and to the extent that they serve as a springboard for a new sense of corporate purpose and renewal. Without previous economic performance the business would not have reached its current position in the environment. But without looking for changing relationships and projecting future achievements, the organization will not be able to survive beyond the present.

Approaches to Entrepreneurial Strategies

CONTINUITY AND CHANGE

Management must always walk a delicate tightrope between continuity and change. In a market economy no stage of change is ever fully completed. In a competitive society people always aspire for greater equality, a higher standard of living and an improved quality of life, making it always an unfinished society. As the leading economic institution of society, the corporation will mirror this incompleteness by striving to satisfy these unfulfilled expectations.

Recognition of the interconnection between continuity and change becomes more feasible as an organizing concept if business decision making is visualized as rotating around three distinct axes: the traditional, the transitional and the transformational. All three dimensions simultaneously call for different degrees of emphasis in the allocation of resources for improved business performance. The traditional business concentrates on the commitments we are making today for the improvement of the current business. The transitional focuses on what will be our commitments today in order to have a tomorrow. In the transformational business we seek new directions for the commitments necessary to assure a different future. Each of these three dimensions raises a distinctively different strategic question. The traditional answers the question, what is our business? The transitional, what will our business be? And the transformational, what should our business be?

The traditional, transitional and transformational dimensions of the business have no separate time locus in the planning process. St. Augustine in *The Confessions* wrestled as perceptively as any thinker in history with the enigma of fleeting time when he concluded that there are three types of time. ". . . yet perchance it might be properly said, there be three times; a present of things past, a present of things present, and a present of things future."[5] All three co-mingle and interpenetrate with each other, ruling out any linear deterministic rationale of time horizons. The entrepreneurial function, however, must integrate the different time spans for each dimension by calculating the time required to make the decision effective, balancing the risks and opportunities, and making allocations for the deployment of people and financial resources. Inevitably, there must be accompanying budgetary tradeoffs based on managerial judgment of how much immediate benefit should be sacrificed for long term results and how much long term expansion should be jeopardized against short range performance. In short, although commitments for all three dimensions are made in the present, the time allowed for each dimension will depend on the length of time calculated to make the entrepreneurial decision effective in terms of economic results. The nature of the business (customer needs and knowledge requirements) and the perceived changes in the environment are the chief determining factors shaping the business time span for each of the three approaches.

The celerity of change in the modern economy leads to one general conclusion about the time element. The time span between initial commitment and economic results is steadily lengthening. As recently as a decade ago an investment in a factory, steel furnace, electrical utility, paper mill, or a telephone plant could count on a payoff within a few years. In today's economy, the time sequence for economic results for those examples is in the neighborhood of ten to fifteen years. The reality of extended duration before the achievement of economic results demands a deeper analysis of the cost of capital and the sophisticated use of capital budgeting techniques than were previously required in periods of relative stability. For instance, Proctor and Gamble has for a long time enjoyed the enviable reputation for speedy product innovation, but it has been estimated that it took ten years and seventy million dollars to bring the Pringle potato chip on the market. The question has also been raised about the wisdom of spending that much money on that type of product.[6]

Moreover, the extended time span associated with an environment in which nothing remains intact for very long means that conditions which may threaten the rationale of the original commitment are constantly changing. The costs involved in entrepreneurial commitments must be allocated in the budget over many years without any assurance of results. Yet, failure to consider the tradeoff between today and tomorrow may mean the demise of the business. In the tradeoff commitment, management must keep the present business healthy or there will be no long run. At the same time, it must see that the business is capable of renewal or else the business will become economically anemic and lose its wealth producing vitality.

The entrepreneurial approach does not mean waiting in the wings for the future to happen and then making a decision. This type of long range planning is futile. Decisions, the future commitments under conditions of uncertainty, are always made in the present, evaporating the artificial distinction between long and short range planning. In effect, long range planning is tantamount to a series of short range decisions. What does the business have to do in today's traditional business to make the transition into tomorrow? And in the longer time horizon, what commitment does management have to make today in order to

Approaches to Entrepreneurial Strategies

transform the business of today into a new mutation, *i.e.*, something entirely distinctive and different? And finally, what will not get done at all if management does not commit resources to it today? Strictly speaking, these are not future decisions; they represent the futurity of present decisions based on what we are going to do now, not in a distant tomorrow.

Different conceptual approaches to decision making are also required for each of the three dimensions. Managing the traditional business entails making the present business better by optimizing the performance of old economic tasks, avoiding what should not be done at all (no matter how efficiently) if it does not contribute to economic results, and seeking out the hidden potential of today's business. Managing the transitional business involves spanning the bridge between continuity and change by skillfully redeploying the current assets of the business and capitalizing on opportunities in the environment. Within the dialectic of continuous business flux, new corporate syntheses emerge in which the successful decisions undertaken on behalf of the transitional business become the routine decisions of tomorrow for a changing traditional business. Managing the transformational business deals with authentic innovation, the effort to create deliberate and purposefully planned change by forging new foundations for a novel business in the future.

Finally, all three dimensions call for different methodologies. The traditional business, the operational, concentrates its main attention on continuity. Although the methodology recognizes the conditioning effects of the past, it is not equated with rigidity but is the realistic recognition of doing better what is already known. The transitional business applies the tools and techniques of risk analysis by assigning probabilities to imaginable opportunities in the environment. If the transitional approach successfully converts problems of uncertainty into economic results by undertaking new projects, it adds a new qualitative mutation to the traditional part of the business. The transformational dimension in trying to invent the future operates in the realm of incalculable uncertainty; consequently, no tools are available. Whereas the first two approaches stress the organization of knowledge, the transformational dimension calls for the organization of ignorance. Within the transformational realm, one works from tomorrow back to today and from today into tomorrow in an interacting circular pattern which has been the model of all great breakthroughs.

To summarize, the management of entrepreneurial change requires the recognition that any business has traditional, transitional and transformational aspects. Each has different characteristics requiring different time, conceptual and methodological approaches. The most important point in understanding the configuration of business change is that all three are organized and related to the total mission of the business. A diagram of interacting circles may help to clarify the hypothesis.

Pattern of Business Change

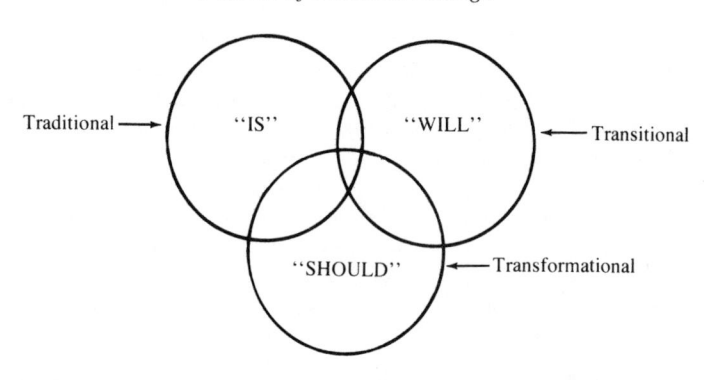

Traditional → "IS"   "WILL" ← Transitional

"SHOULD" ← Transformational

A biological organism is limited to one biography to a customer. An artificial entity, such as a corporation, can successfully transcend the biological life span (the traditional) by providing for sequels in the form of new alternative hypothetical biographies (the transitional) and a radically new biography for the future (the transformational).

Illustration of Corporate Change: Sears Roebuck's Strategic Decisions

Additional insight into the concept of a corporation having overlapping but distinct biographies becomes clearer when one traces the qualitative decisions of great companies in responding to changing environmental realities. Sears Roebuck and Company, for example, founded by Richard Sears started out not too differently from scores of other businesses by selling watches through catalogues. Julius Rosenwald in the late eighteen nineties committed the company to winning the trust of the farmer by guaranteeing money back if the customer was not satisfied. He assured warranty at a fair price by constructing a mail order plant with strict quality control. He also deposited money in Postal Savings to back up the company's claim of reliability.

Meanwhile the company was developing appropriate manufacturing and purchasing skills to translate into practice the objective of acting as the buying agent for the middle class household. General Robert Wood in the nineteen twenties maintained that Sears made every mistake possible, but fortunately saw the importance of the automobile in changing rural and suburban America. He launched the company on a building spree of retail stores creating the nucleus of today's shopping mall. Add to these such additional entrepreneurial decisions as: Allstate Insurance Company, foreign expansion, management development, and social responsibility, and we get a clearer view of the different biographical mutations in Sears Roebuck's past. All these great strategic decisions simultaneously enlarged the base of successful retailing and extended the life of the business. The growth pattern, moreover, is irreversible; no amount of magic could ever again convert the Sears Roebuck Company into a small business. In responding successfully to new opportunities in the environment, it added new chapters of growth, prolonged its existence and altered its mission. Sears Roebuck, along with other great enterprises, mirrored, by their strategic decisions, the shaping of new corporate identities and helped assure them a multi-volume biography on the shelf of business history.

Because growth is such an elusive phenomenon, a deeper exploration of the characteristics of the traditional, transitional and transformational characteristics requires elaboration.

THE TRADITIONAL BUSINESS

The Claims of the Past

In most large corporations the present range of products and services will, in all likelihood, shape the identity of the business in the immediate future. It is most likely that in the next few years such companies as Sears Roebuck, International Business Machines, United States Steel, General Electric, and other corporations will be marketing a substantial number of the same products and services being offered by them today. Joseph Schumpeter alluded to this feature of continuity in discussing economic development when he stated: "Thus the economic system will not change conspicuously on its own initiative, but will at all times be connected with the present state of affairs. This may be called Wieser's principles of continuity."[7]

Complacency of Success

One of the difficulties executives have in handling the identity crisis of the traditional business is that everyday familiarity within the business (the factor of continuity) tends to breed arrogance. This is particularly true when many managements are not consciously aware of the qualitative reasons for their past business success. It is in the nature of things that because people are working hard and achieving reasonable economic results in the traditional business they become over-confident and lulled into a sense of complacency. Too often, however, the confidence stems from a mistaken conviction that the original entrepreneurial decision which built the business will last forever. Meanwhile, operating problems inevitably arise which are actually symptoms that management has not diagnosed its identity in a thoroughly perceptual and conceptual manner. When the problems turn into genuine crises, a loss of faith in the stable state of the traditional business looms ominously. The pressures from day-to-day events blur the reality of future needs. In concentrating on doing things routinely, instead of thinking things through, planning is subverted by putting the cart before the horse.

The railroads are perhaps the classic example of an industry fighting unsuccessfully to maintain the traditional steady state. By rigidly and narrowly defining their business as railroads instead of transportation, management mistakenly believed that the regulatory agencies would afford a cartelized umbrella of protection against the risk of external competitive forces. Meanwhile, technology was creating new forms of transportation (automobile, truck, aeroplane, etc.) which altered customer wants and eroded the market dominance of the railroads. More specifically, the diesel and its accompanying featherbedding problem illustrates railroad management's misdiagnosis of technological change. The diesel engine, which challenged the steam locomotive in the mid-nineteen thirties, was virtually forced upon the railroad industry as a result of marketing pressure and initial subsidization by General Motors.

The inability of the railroads to recognize the diesel as a major innovation hoisted a featherbedding albatross around the neck of the industry. When railroad management agreed in its labor negotiations to accept the unnecessary man in the diesel cab rather than replace the fireman, management visualized the diesel as a fad, which at best, would be limited to its commuter lines, the smallest segment of the business. In failing to recognize the technological superiority of the diesel over the steam locomotive, railroad management made the mistake of responding in a routine tactical manner instead of instituting a new labor strategy to fit the reality of the diesel. After more than a generation of bitter negotiations with the union, the issue still has not been fully resolved.

Business Purpose—First Planning Need

The first and obvious guideline of planning is to determine business purpose. Assuming the obvious is not characteristically a human trait, and for most people the failing is not too dangerous; but, when people reach positions of power and responsibility taking things for granted is a perilous and myopic luxury. Stimulation for achievement emerges from defining corporate identity. In examining the enterprise for its strengths in markets, in people and in other resources within the traditional business, management is actually looking backward into the future, enabling it to obtain a greater measure of control over its destiny.

A common denominator of mediocre and marginal businesses is the amount of energy expended in trying to keep their heads above water. Of course, it is important for managers to avoid sinking into the depths of bankruptcy; but, at the same time, exclusive concern with staying afloat presents difficulties in steering the corporate ship beyond the horizons of traditional waters and into the new transitional seas. Neil Chamberlain, Professor of Business Administration, Columbia Graduate School of Business, expands on the nautical metaphor in the following way: "The captain of a sinking ship does not spend his time planning his destination, on the other hand, the captain who does not plan his destination may find himself in charge of a sinking ship."[8]

Power of Tradition

Recognizing the claims of the past and the demands of the future is a far easier task than finding methods for implementing these dual imperatives. One of the difficulties is the belief held by many in the permanence of the traditional business. This belief, which frequently becomes obsessional, operates against the management of change and provides a bureaucratic cushion against recognizing uncertainty. The contention, however, that it is possible to remain the same is illusory. Except for natural monopolies, security blankets are not standard equipment in any business. At the same time, the tenacity of the non-innovators eating at the "cake of custom" inevitably emerges when entrepreneurial efforts are made to introduce change.

A&P is a case in point of a company becoming a prisoner of tradition, despite its ability to hold the number one position in the food retail industry for decades. Its dominance throughout this period, however, was largely attributable to the potency of the original entrepreneurial decisions by its founders, the Hartford brothers. Because managing change effectively was not a company strength, A&P accepted the innovation of the supermarket belatedly and reluctantly. As it expanded to over 4,000 store units, it failed to sustain an entrepreneurial fervor among its managers on the branch level. By inbreeding a top management of elderly senior executives, it encouraged a pattern of organizational incest; displaying an almost pathological resistance to abandoning marginal and mediocre stores. Finally, it resorted to an unsophisticated tactic of price slashing, while at the same time allowing its service to deteriorate in countering its recent competition. In the hope of once again attaining the number one position, A&P has broken with tradition by hiring a chief executive officer from the outside and abandoning about one-third of its stores. In a recent newspaper report A&P's net income doubled in the third fiscal period of 1976. It is still too early, however, to determine whether this is because of a tax credit or improved managerial performance.

According to Donald Schon, a prominent management consultant, the supporters of the traditional steady state will practice "dynamic conservatism" through such tactics as reinforcement and co-option in blunting innovating efforts. Whether such reactionary tactics are maliciously or subconsciously contrived is irrelevant. They are doomed to disappointment as the eruption of critical problems confuses objectives, smothers identity and, indeed, threatens the very belief in the existence of the traditional stationary state. As the steady state increasingly deteriorates, people within the business have a difficult time communicating among themselves. The Rashomon effect, based on a popular Japanese movie which depicted the multiple interpretations of a single event by various participants, takes place when managers fail to perceive for what knowledge the business is really being paid and what the customer thinks is value. The business that loses its strategic sense of mission by failing to define itself clearly is not likely to do well in the long run.[9]

Defining the Business—Quest For Corporate Identity

Faced with the problems of inevitable crises, if it follows the paths of drift and inertia, how can the corporation accommodate to change without losing the bonds of continuity? And in the midst of explosive events in which the luxury of time for accommodation to change is increasingly dwindling, how can the corporation evoke constructive responses while maintaining dynamic equilibrium? Answering these questions is impossible without raising a more fundamental question: What is our business? Ascertaining corporate identity or what we really stand for is a demanding intellectual task. Consequently, except among most sophisticated managements, the question is seldom raised and rarely answered.

The Mirage of Product Definition

In searching for corporate identity a frequent source of confusion emerges when a business is defined in terms of a product. More often than not such an approach is an exercise in futility. Defining a business in generic terms (we manufacture clothes, for example) contributes little to the fabrication of corporate identity. The making of clothes implies an internal view, assuming that the business is definable from the inside.

Starting out with an inside approach of what we think the business is instead of considering the customer's view of utility is likely to be a diagnosis which is wrong as well as irrelevant. The making of clothes is simply a vehicle, which fails to clarify what the business does and what it does not do. Within the internal boundaries of the business, no values are created. Looking at the business from the inside focuses on quantitative areas of costs, efforts and problems; it neglects the qualitative arenas of knowledge and the customer. The internal approach, moreover, is silent in the critical areas of what is not our business.

To determine the nature of a business more clearly, an examination of customer needs is required and the unique knowledge excellences of the business must be rigorously diagnosed. The key result area of a clothing business, for example, may reside in converting of raw or synthetic material into finished goods, providing mass distribution, pioneering of style or fashion, selling the concept of beautiful people, adapting or copying of style for a segmented market. Or, it may be a combination of several such factors, depending on how management allocates its resources in the achievement of economic results. In the same industry individual companies may do many functional things competently, but it is only possible for them to do a few unique things superbly, reaffirming the principle that there is never a single way to develop a mass market.

Defining the business exclusively in broad generic terms (clothing, shoes, automobiles, supermarkets, paper, etc.) fails to provide any clue to understanding real corporate strengths and managerial commitments. Although there is always a peril in defining business strategy too narrowly in terms of a special knowledge excellence in fulfilling customer needs, it does provide an initial appraisal of what the customer thinks is value and for what knowledge he is paying the enterprise. No product has any utility until a customer decides to exchange his purchasing power for it; he is not concerned with how hard the company is working but only in what he perceives the product can do for him. No product has economic utility unless somebody buys it. As Theodore Levitt noted: "Last year consumers bought one million one quarter inch bits, but not because they perceived the need for bits but they wanted one quarter inch holes."[10]

The Concept of Knowledge Excellence

Successful businesses have eluded the alluring siren of product enchantment by defining their enterprises uniquely in terms of the customer value system and their own knowledge excellences. Countless examples indicate how certain firms have transcended the narrow boundary of product definition by concentrating on a unique knowledge excellence to meet customer needs. Among the most prominent success stories are the following:

—Sears Roebuck & Company visualized one of its great strengths as becoming the purchasing agent of the middle class family. By intimately familiarizing itself with the tastes of middle class America, it controls the design of the products purchased by its Chicago headquarters in the merchandising mix of its stores.

—Marks and Spencer, the great English retailing firm, concentrated on elevating the tastes of the British lower classes. Through the innovation of mass distribution and quality control throughout Britain, it consciously set out to democratize the economy by making available upper class goods for lower class customers.

—McDonald's Corporation went beyond the conventional hamburger business by developing a systems analysis approach centering on speedy service, decent food and cleanliness. In effect, it overcame what was considered insurmountable obstacles by skillfully introducing mass production assembly line techniques into the service area.

—Revlon, Inc. sold the value added of hope rather than perfume *per se*. Charles Revson was acutely aware of the role customer expectation played in the marketing of his products. Realizing the consumer expected to pay higher prices for luxury items sold in fashionable outlets, he rejected the principle of a small marginal mark-up over costs. For glamor products with elaborate packaging the female customer was willing to pay more or else she could have purchased virtually the same product in a five and dime store.

—O. M. Scott and Sons saw its business not in traditional grass seeds but in the matrix of lawn care. It developed the knowledge to implement this excellence in agronomy, pesticides and special lawn tools.

—Gerber Products, Inc. stressed nutrition in marketing baby foods. It hired professional nutritionists in the field of pediatrics and emphasized it was second to none in satisfying the health food needs of the baby.

—J. C. Penney Company, Incorporated innovated in the area of "space economy" in retailing its products. It recognized that unused store space was an unproductive cost, and proceeded to view the segments of store space as potential profit centers.

—International Chemical Corporation developed a special excellence in consulting services for the promotion of its products. It encouraged its customers to take advantage of its unique knowledge by utilizing its salesmen to solve business problems.

—Nabisco, Inc. recognized the critical importance of supermarket shelf space for its business. By arranging with the supermarket for the allocation of a small percentage of shelf space to be assigned exclusively to Nabisco, it then developed special distribution strength among its salesforce for shelving and display. As a result the customer was assured of fresh products and the retailer was assured that the Nabisco corner of the store would always be adequately stocked.

—Anheuser-Busch Incorporated committed itself to the recreation industry as a vehicle for franchising beer. For a more detailed treatment of its special excellence, see pages 74 and 75.

—Campbell Soup Company perceptively recognized the importance of categorizing its market into two principal segments (the ultimate consumer and the retailer). It deployed its resources in both directions. First, the company conducted high level advertising and promotional campaigns to attract the consumer; and, second, its staff arranged training programs in supervisory techniques for the benefit of the supermarket employees and its retail customers.

—General Foods Corporation allocated a substantial portion of its resources to market research in determining the broad spectrum of consumer wants. It developed a special capacity for broad segmentation of coffee to suit the major class segments and tastes in the market.

—International Business Machines Corporation bills for hardware but prides itself in knowing more about the customer's information needs than the customer does. It has applied the task concept of marketing in which the salesman and the engineer jointly participate in preparing a plan for data processing and in providing the office equipment tools for the knowledge worker.

—Kimberly Clark Corporation pushed the value added concept of sanitation in the sale of its paper products. The company accidently discovered that nurses during World War I used hospital cotton for menstrual purposes. Subsequently, in introducing its own paper products, it has never forgotten the original insight of the role of sanitation in marketing its products.

—The Maytag Company is a profit leader in the highly competitive electrical appliance industry. It has traditionally chalked up nearly triple the earnings in sales of its competitors. Maytag's special excellence is a commitment to high quality engineering. As a result of providing this unique value to its customers, it is able to charge approximately $100 more for its appliances than its competitors. Moreover, it reinforces this quality image by avoiding private labels and controlling its distribution through a selected network of independent dealers.

Most of the companies mentioned are leaders in their respective industries. As mentioned previously, however, there is never a single answer in meeting the needs of a mass market. In the quest for special excellence, every successful company will provide different answers resulting in different types of companies with different management styles. At one time, for example, Alcoa, Coca Cola and General Electric (light bulb division) were approaching a quasi-monopolistic market position. Meanwhile, competitors concentrating on other ways of serving the customer and developing their own unique knowledge capabilities obtained a greater share of the market as well as enlarging the total market. Despite a declining proportion of the market Alcoa, Coca Cola, and the General Electric Company continued to grow in absolute terms, proving the value of healthy competition as a force for good in society.

The Mystique of Success

Another difficulty facing even the most outstanding companies in defining the business clearly is the danger of being hypnotized by overwhelming success. Success is not a final answer. For in the wake of

Approaches to Entrepreneurial Strategies

success emerge new problems and opportunities which erode many of the former conditions of success. What was considered business excellence at one stage in the traditional business can quickly assume the characteristics of a restraining incubus. Only in romantic Hollywood do people live happily ever after. Because events within and outside the business refuse to remain stationary, any company rigorously wedded to past success is inviting potential extinction. In entrepreneurial thinking the consumer is always, and quite properly, raising the unsentimental question, "What have you done for me lately?"

Need For Increasing Effectiveness Of Traditional Business

Although the starting point for managing change is within the confines of the traditional business, it is a fallacy to assume that the present business is performing up to peak potential. A sounder and more frank admission is that many of today's operations are being performed incompetently. No business organization is exempt from the second law of thermodynamics which dictates the inevitable fostering of waste, friction and misallocation of resources. Unless a business can modify the phenomenon of ubiquitous entropy, which is constantly running the system down, it will face serious handicaps in meeting the challenge of change. The continual care and feeding of problems, at the expense of opportunities, will quickly produce a famine in resources.

A most pressing task within the traditional business is to make the current activities more effective by reducing waste. If the task is accomplished with increased competency, additional resources will be available to meet the uncertainties of tomorrow. In assuming, moreover, that an untapped potential for improved performance exists, the business earns the accompanying dividend that a more positive attitude toward change will be fostered, dispelling the notion that the decisions of the traditional business are blocked in granite. Fortunately, the path to achievement in this area is not entirely uncharted. The experiences of many successful businesses have evolved putative principles capable of being translated into action. A number of these diagnostic and tactical tools will be discussed in a subsequent section on techniques.

THE TRANSITIONAL BUSINESS

Challenge of New Commitments

If present activity is the operational heart of the traditional business, current projects dealing with new commitments constitute the brain function of the transitional business. Decisions within traditional business, originally novel and entrepreneurial, rapidly become procedural and routine. Although it is important to recognize the role that the past plays in conditioning the future, it is also imperative to recognize the need for future strategic decisions to escape obsolescence. The regularities of the past are crucial in the short run, but unless we assume a steady state existence they are eventually meaningless in shaping a new sense of purpose to determine what the business intends to become. The relationship between the traditional and transitional stages of the business will always be characterized by an uneasy balance between past and present, continuity and change, cohesion and disturbance, and the need for stability, on the one hand, and dynamic disequilibrium on the other.

Dynamic Tensions of Becoming

In an environment of convulsive change the tension between the traditional and transitional dimensions of the business becomes increasingly acute. Every business undergoes a continual identity crisis in response to these changes. United States Steel Corporation's business is no longer exclusively relegated to the production of steel. In order to meet the needs of its customers, who are usually unconcerned about the physical components of the product as long as it performs for them, United States Steel devotes approximately fifty percent of its production to non-steel items, for example, cement and plastic products. In determining what it intends to become, every business is forced to think through future alternatives and potential achievements. The intellectual task is to identify future alternatives; the commitment task is to concentrate on those producing the greatest economic results.

Chief Task—Focus on New Opportunities

Consequently, the chief task for the transitional business is to supplement the traditional business foundation by focusing on new opportunities in response to external stimuli and by imaginatively utilizing internal corporate strengths. In the process of deploying resources toward improved economic performance the concern within the transitional milieu does not center on any single strategic decision. The decision making pattern is one of a cluster of many incremental commitments, some obviously more important than others. In a practical sense, management is often acting as a juggler, dropping some projects and adding others as corporate pressures dictate. The key in discerning the amount of forward development in the transitional business is to examine the budget allocation for such projects as: new products, entry into new markets, introduction of new financial systems, public relations, merger and acquisition programs, new plant facilities, marketing research, corporate reorganization and training and management development.

The transitional business is in constant flux. Management must endeavor to achieve a new state of dynamic equilibrium, directed away from the traditional business by focusing on future expectations, future potential realities and future economic performance. At the same time, management, in seeking new opportunities and attempting to improve performance by undertaking new projects, must be acutely aware that the totality of these incremental decisions may be qualitatively altering the mission of the business. An illustration is the Columbia Broadcasting System search for new opportunities outside its traditional fields of radio and television which led the company into the areas of publishing and baseball. In the process of becoming a mini-conglomerate, it was losing its identity. The danger in the CBS case is that a company can define itself too narrowly (i.e., broadcasting) and miss out on opportunities· but, it can also define itself too broadly (i.e., entertainment) and cloud its mission.

In any event, despite the difficulties connected with selecting opportunities, management, within the transitional business dimension, must not only endure change it must also court it. Whereas the traditional business concentrates on making yesterday's commitments more effective, the transitional business focuses on becoming (i.e. the corporate commitment of allocating current scarce resources to an uncertain future) in order to assure that there will be a business tomorrow. As an entrepreneurial strategy it recognizes that the business has no choice but to convert itself to the future. Undertaking the entrepreneurial task means rejecting the mindless response and accepting the challenge of managing change systematically.

Coping With Uncertainty—Techniques

Textbooks on planning discuss a number of techniques for coping with uncertainty. Among the most prominent are: the Delphi Method, Program Evaluation Review Technique, game theory and simulation models. The quantitative approach has its place, but it should follow and not precede the conceptualization of business conduct and behavior. Its importance resides more in the implementation of the decision than in diagnosis. In predicting future reality, the quantitative approach has severe limitations. The case of statistical forecasting serves to illustrate the point.

Statistical Forecasting

Forecasts are useful and indispensable in organizing economic intelligence but can turn into disasters if acted upon literally and not monitored for the unexpected. Forecasting, in effect, tells us what has already happened. It is basically an extrapolation of yesterday. In general, forecasting is most reliable in the area of demographics. But in other areas, given the static premises of *ceteris paribus*, forecasts fail to encompass the discontinuity or break in the linear or serial pattern. Failure to take into account the unique event which qualitatively alters the pattern is not meant to belittle the achievements of the statisticians and management scientists, but rather to cite the difficulty connected with the use of the forecasting tool. Few companies, for example, can equal the talents of the professional statisticians in the New York Telephone Company. However, their predictions of telephone usage in the early sixties went astray and threatened the functioning of the entire network in New York City. The forecast had no way of depicting the exponential growth of trading on the stock market, the unexpected pressure for telephones resulting from an increase in the welfare rolls, and the vulnerabilities created by crime and vandalism. The forecasts were statistically valid, but increasingly irrelevant, because it was impossible for anybody to predict the three discontinuities. Forecasting is an important tool but it is not an omnipotent one. From an entrepreneurial point of view it has severe limitations.

Futurology

Special mention has been noted earlier of the alleged discipline of futurology, the latest effort to predict what the world will look like ten or twenty years hence. Assuming the new "think tanks" can fathom the mysteries of changing environment, the task of the businessman coping with uncertainty would be simplified. Reading the voluminous literature of the futurologists will produce insights into the general scenario of future change, but placing entrepreneurial bets on the predictions of the futurologists is a highly riskful enterprise. The irony of prediction is that despite its miserable performance, the increased uncertainty of our times dictates a greater demand for forecasting services. Eric Hoffer, the San Francisco longshoreman who has become a celebrated social philosopher, comments on this addiction for knowing the future when he states: "It is a paradox that in our time of rapid drastic change, when the future is in our midst devouring the present before our eyes, we have never been less certain of what is ahead of us."[11]

Because the track record for prediction is so undistinguished, reflections about future outcomes should always accompany a substantial dosage of humility. A cursory examination of some of the most outstanding breakthroughs in scientific and technological history reveals that even the most brilliant minds had major blindspots. For example, Galileo, father of astronomy, failed to comprehend the significance of atmospheric pressure; Joseph Priestley, the English chemist, ignored the chemical contributions of the pioneer of chemistry, Antoine Lavoisier; Simon Newcomb, generally recognized as the most eminent American scientist of his day, flatly predicted a few weeks before the Wright Brothers' flight that such a feat was impossible; Thomas Edison, for all his undisputed genius, for almost a generation rejected the feasibility of alternating current; Lord William Thomson Kelvin, the British physicist, considered Roentgen's x-rays a hoax because they did not lend themselves to proper scientific measurement; and, despite Lord Ernest Rutherford's great contributions to physics, he maintained that the splitting of the atom was an impossibility. Finally, during World War II American Admiral William Leahy rendered his assessment of the "Manhattan project" for the creation of the atom bomb as: "This is the biggest fool thing we have ever done. The atomic bomb will never go off, and I speak as an expert on explosives."[12]

The point is, of course, if such great minds had difficulty in perceiving innovation in their own field, then the task of prediction for the non-specialist businessman is even more overwhelming in determining the impact of technological change. It is important to recognize that two decades ago most businessmen underestimated the massive commercial expansion of the computer, failed to see the rise of franchising, and neglected to forecast the growth of conglomerates. Moreover, with regard to the social impact of technology, no one foresaw that DDT, in destroying pesty bugs, would also take its toll on the bees fertilizing the fruit orchards and produce harmful side effects in humans. Nobody predicted that public health and sanitation improvements in the less developed world would result in pressing demographic problems; nobody prognosticated that the pharmaceutical breakthrough in antibiotics would also trigger the rise of a dangerous drug culture; and, nobody perceived that the birth control pill would foster a sexual revolution.

Weakness of Futurology

The farther out into the future the futurologists predict, the more diminishing are prospects of success. Moreover, in formulating their technological assessments they remain prisoners of today's cultural realities, making it almost impossible to perceive the new inventions in an altered social pattern. H. G. Wells, a futurologist par excellence, around the turn of the century, brilliantly foresaw many of the technological accomplishments of the twentieth century. In making his predictions in an Edwardian cultural milieu, however, he was unable to discern the social impact of his prophecies. Since the invention alters and is altered by the value system, there is no way of market researching a genuinely new product. Futurology has its place in fueling the imagination, but drawing pretty lines on charts for enactment at some future date is a futile form of planning. There are no future decisions; there is only the futurity of present ones. Where a company will be in 1980 depends on the commitments made today.[13]

Future—What We Know About It For Certain

The only thing we can say about the future with certainty is that it will be different. The only fact for sure about the future is that there are no facts, only expectations. The future, however, is not deterministic. Its being unformed means that it can be shaped to a considerable degree by today's entrepreneurial commitment. Paradoxically, the assumption that the future cannot be predicted makes the argument for planning all the more imperative.

Testing Underlying Assumptions

As noted previously, management, in planning for change must think through the risks and opportunities occurring in the present environment. If commitments are made to opportunities, and the new projects are successful in their aggregate, they will provide the business with a new sense of purpose. In the transitional phase of the business, change is the norm and continuity is the exception. The chief underlying strategic assumption is that the assumptions of the traditional stationary state are no longer true. H. L. Gantt, one of the pioneers of scientific management, made the comment: "The usual way of doing things is the wrong way."[14] One may not have to accept Gantt's thesis fully, but, at the very least, he has an obligation to test assumptions against current realities and future expectations. Such an approach not only has the benefit of conceding that things will be different, but is also related to the difficult assignment of questioning one's success.

Management's Perception of Environment Determines Direction

Consequently, managers must make rigorous assumptions about business realities, particularly in the external environment. The manner in which management interprets the environment molds its direction. For instance, the House of Branfi, the sole importer of Riunite wine, looked at the drinking patterns of the youth market in the early sixties. Management saw them drinking an amber colored, carbonated, sweet cola liquid. Consequently, it began the importation of an amber colored, carbonated, semi-sweet Lambrusca wine. Today Riunite is the largest single imported wine in the United States.

The more the manager is attached to the objectives of the traditional business, the more his developing obsession with facts and figures increases his reluctance to look outside. The internal vision prevails because it is the most easily quantified. A preponderant amount of business quantification is misleading because it reflects problems and efforts at the expense of results. Knowledge and the customers are the key performance sectors; everything else is cost. Put another way, the customer pays for revenue, everything else is cost.

The internal perception, moreover, omits the true test of a social institution which is its specific contribution to society and the individual. Thus, its real purpose lies outside its organizational boundaries. All social institutions are nourished from the outside, making it mandatory for management to construct sensing mechanisms for probing the qualitative trends affecting the business. Specifically, managing the transitional stage of the business demands a knowledge of the qualitative and irreversible forces affecting the knowledge core and customer needs, which in turn, will alter the societal mission of the business. The modern corporation, with all its limitations, is the best organizational instrument available to accomplish this purpose. If, however, it fails to serve society, it can be eliminated and replaced by society. What society gives, society can also take away.

Environmental Restraints

External uncertainties are beyond the control of any business. In addition to the social pressures threatening all institutions, the customer can deny his purchasing power to any business. Moreover, knowledge, the mental capital of modern industry, has two key characteristics—impermanence and general availability. In short, immediately upon making its appearance, it is already becoming obsolete and as a social resource others can readily take advantage of it. Even the mighty American Telephone and Telegraph Corporation, the classic monopoly, is being challenged by a swarm of buzzing entrepreneurs who are offering new communication services by adopting the pioneering technology of the Bell System. Paradoxically, it was the introduction of the transistor by Bell Laboratories which triggered a revolution in communications, and, at the same time, undermined the foundations of the company's knowledge monopoly.

Knowledge as Protection Against Surprise

Increased knowledge of the environment enables the manager to obtain greater confidence in avoiding surprise and to recognize future possibilities in planning. In trying to make sense of what is taking place in the turbulent external sector, where future facts are nonexistent and past regularities assume diminishing importance, management is faced with the difficult challenge of responding to a social reality it can neither fully grasp nor totally understand. If management is not slightly confused in today's complex and rapidly changing environment, it is only reacting and not thinking. As mentioned previously, because the quantitative tools emphasize validity at the expense of relevance, they have serious limitations. The proper place for technique is after diagnosis.

Role of Anticipation

Anticipation is the future the manager expects to happen. Although there are no real facts in the future, except for the logical positivist, expectations are far from illusory. Expectations become significantly meaningful, if the manager commits resources to them and if they are subsequently translated into economic results.

At the same time, wagering on what one expects to happen, while often sound, remains a venturesome endeavor. There are countless entrepreneurial success stories documenting that an individual can be brilliantly right, but business history records a larger number of cases proving that one can also be brilliantly wrong. Anticipation is heavily subjective and usually runs counter to the conventional wisdom in not taking things for granted. Anticipation is important because it avoids the danger of overrationalization in the planning process. Elements of non-logical thinking are important if only because the quantitative tools of management science are more concerned with validity than relevance.

The twilight zone between logical and non-logical thinking was succinctly stated by the English author, G. K. Chesterton: "The real trouble with the world of ours is not that it is an unreasonable world, not even that it is a reasonable one. The commonest kind of trouble is that it is nearly reasonable, but not quite. Life is not an illogicality; yet it is a trap for logicians. It looks just a little more mathematical and regular than it is; its exactitude is obvious, but its inexactitude is hidden; its wilderness lies in wait."[15] Chesterton's words are a reminder that in any entrepreneurial strategy a place for a proportionate amount of relevant imagination should always exist.

The Recent Past—Projection

In identifying external relevance for business opportunities and economic results, projection, the attempt to depict those changes which have already arrived in society, but whose impacts have not fully registered on the business, is another important analytical tool. In essence, projection is the future that has already happened, and by virtue of incipient occurrence, is already undermining the existence of the traditional business.

Environmental Audit

In a complex interdependent society a cynic may conclude that everything taking place within the environment influences the business; but, when everything is relevant, nothing, paradoxically, is actually relevant. Moreover, each business is *sui generis*. The relevant environment of any business is defined partly by its present activities and partly by its preparedness to consider new activities in achieving results. The strategic mission of each business dictates management's interpretation of social forces and its response to environmental impacts. Depending on the business, some trends will affect the business only peripherally, whereas others may threaten the survival, unless converted, into direct economic opportunities.

In his study on entrepreneurship, Kirzner points out the importance of knowledge being alert to external forces:

> Ultimately, then, the kind of knowledge required for entrepreneurship is "knowing where to look for knowledge" rather than knowledge of substantive market information. The word which most closely captures this kind of "knowledge" seems to be *alertness*. It is true that alertness may be hired; but one who hires an employee alert to the possibilities of discovering knowledge has himself displayed alertness of a still higher order. Entrepreneurial knowledge may be described as the highest order of knowledge, the ultimate knowledge needed to harness available information already possessed (or capable of being possessed).[16]

In using the analytical tool of projection to conduct an environmental audit each firm will have to do individual homework. However, all firms will have to draw specific conclusions from the canvas of American society. The corporation is both a creator and creature of change. From the point of view of systems theory, the corporation in adjusting to states of dynamic equilibrium is continually conducting countless transactions with the social, political and economic forces in the environment. Depending on how management responds, the environmental forces may become threats to corporate survival or they may be converted into business opportunities. In the present era it is unlikely that businessmen can continue to be economic revolutionaries while remaining conservative when it comes to the quality of life.

In one fashion or another management must take into account in its projection analysis such trends as:

— demographic changes

- the organizational revolution
- middle-class society
- the political and regulatory climate
- post-industrial society
- the education explosion and the knowledge revolution
- the black revolt
- the women's movement
- the youth rebellion and the counter culture
- ecology
- degenerative societal problems (unemployment, work alienation, recession, inflation, etc.)
- social responsibility
- the problems of corporate authority and legitimacy
- the social and economic needs of the elderly
- the shifting role of the labor union
- the international environment
- the changing value system.

The list is far from complete, but even such a limited scenario deflates arrogance and induces sober humility for any management coming to grips with so diverse a pattern of interacting complexity under conditions of uncertainty. In trying to eliminate potential surprise through a systematic projection analysis of the social forces affecting the business, management must recognize that in an era of radical change even the most exhaustive environmental audit is bound to be incomplete, unsure, and potentially wrong in terms of business relevance.

The defunct automobile, the Edsel, is perhaps a classic example of over-systematizing the market research function. It is also the perfect illustration of the exactly right product appearing on the market at the wrong time. By the early nineteen fifties, apparently as a reflection of growing consumer affluence, the middle class car (Pontiac, Oldsmobile, Buick) was gaining marketing momentum. It seemed that the middle class car, the so-called "People's Cadillac," would replace Chevrolet and Ford from the one-two market position. However, by the time the Ford Company brought the Edsel on the market, the customer had shifted his buying strategy from segmentation (a purchaser for every purse) to the personal car based on individual life styles. The subsequent success of the Buick Riviera, the Oldsmobile Tornado, Cadillac Eldorado, and of course, the Ford Mustang, can all be attributed to this fundamental change from class to style in consumer wants.

Subjective uncertainty will be the permanent frame of mind for the entrepreneur. But this has always been and always will be the *modus operandi* of the entrepreneur. By systematizing the task in conducting a learning dialogue with the environment, he can develop greater confidence by pushing reason as far as possible and thereby improve his prospects for success through increased knowledge.

THE TRANSFORMATIONAL BUSINESS

Admission of Ignorance— A Prerequisite

All the previous discussion about managing change confirms the contention that the future will not yield its mysteries automatically. The issue of uncertainty is even more pronounced when we attempt to invent the future for the transformational dimension of the business. As Jean Jacques Rousseau, the French philosopher and social reformer, reminds us: "The ability to foresee that some things cannot be foreseen is a very necessary quality." The greatest president in American history, Abraham Lincoln, recognized this reality when he said: "I confess plainly that I have not controlled events, events have controlled me."

Instead of evoking a stubborn reluctance to express ignorance, admission of ignorance is the first requirement in converting the business into something new and different. On this point, Eric Hoffer once noted: "When a situation is so unprecedented that no amount of knowledge or experience is adequate to master it, then the ignorant and inexperienced are more fit to deal with it than the learned or experienced. The unknown and the untried give as it were a special fitness for the unfit."[17]

Organizing Ignorance

Hoffer has a point, but it can be pushed too far. In areas where no real discernible trends exist, great breakthroughs are possible. The admission of ignorance is futile unless courageously acted upon in making entrepreneurial decisions. Success stories such as the polio vaccine, transistor, DNA molecule, the inter-ballistic missile program, penicillin, the Manhattan Project, the National Aeronautics and Space Administration program and others all suggest, at least to a limited degree, that it is possible to organize ignorance systematically. The strict methodology of imaginatively writing down expectations about the unknown, then

Approaches to Entrepreneurial Strategies

working back to the present, and finally, checking results through feedback has been the common denominator of all the previously cited innovations. In this sense, then, it is feasible to have a subject matter in a discipline where no facts exist.

In all of the examples mentioned, the conventional wisdom and codified knowledge were insufficient for a breakthrough. As a matter of fact because a new intellectual paradigm was required, the old knowledge was more of a hindrance than an asset. A closer look at one of these illustrations, the inter-ballistic missile program, will help to illuminate the point of a new approach for organizing ignorance.

In the early nineteen fifties when the inter-ballistic missile program was initially contemplated, four major areas of theoretical ignorance (fuel, guidance, re-entry and warhead) had to be overcome. Without solving all four, no full fledged missile system was possible. When Vanevaar Bush, one of the most eminent American scientists and one of the fathers of the atomic bomb, confronted the project, he estimated that the solution of the fuel problem alone, necessary to send the missiles into space, would require thirty to forty years. Indeed, if the missile problem was attacked on a linear vector method of working in the four areas independently, the problem may have been insoluble.

But, by applying the analytical tool of systems planning, rough time estimates of the four principal vectors were projected into the future. Then, by using a critical path analysis, the planners were able to monitor the four areas interdependently as a total system. In each of the other breakthrough cases cited, the same common denominator of planning was present. Each breakthrough started with a similar ambiguous solution, with the innovators again working backward in a non-linear fashion toward a successful completion.

Purposefully Planned Change

Inventing the future in which no visible trends exist is a relatively new task for the businessman. When one expected the future to remain relatively stable, then concern for innovation as a priority task was unimportant. Yet when one thinks about it, since only the future is unformed, the only place where the businessman can make an impact is in the future. As an old Chinese proverb states: "If people do not attend to the future, they will soon have to attend to the present."

The examples cited in the organization of ignorance segment are of such complexity that they transcend ordinary business risk. Perhaps the approximate example in the field of business of organizing ignorance for purposefully planned change was the pioneering entrepreneurial vision of Henry Ford. Economic history textbooks typically honor Ford for his innovation of mass production; actually, all he did was refine this technique for automobiles.

A more important contribution was Ford's entrepreneurial mission of putting America on wheels by providing a car that every working man could afford. At a time when the automobile was considered a rich man's toy, the conventional wisdom of the day would have labeled it "an impossible dream." By instituting mass production methods, the five dollar a day wage and denying stockholders immediate dividends, Ford was actually working backward in order to translate his great goal into reality. But equally important, Ford shrewdly perceived that price alone does not create a market, but that a market also creates a demand. The market, in effect, would trigger the demand once he created a car for approximately three hundred sixty five dollars.

What Should Our Business Be?

As mentioned earlier, the future is not a matter of resigned surrender to some predetermined order. Providing that management exercises a wise stewardship of present resources and makes commitment to new opportunities, the future can be shaped to some degree. In most instances, however, the future demands more than the rhetorical lip service it frequently gets. The fact is we just don't have to talk about the future; we can do something about it. At the very least we can raise relevant questions about the requirements for converting the business into something new and different.

The key question for the transformational business is "what should the business be?" In going beyond the conception of "being" in the traditional business and the notion of "becoming" in the transitional business, the transformational concentrates on the novel and innovative by focusing on what we would ideally like to become in the future. In making a leap into the unknown by making a commitment today, the task is to change the purpose and mission of the business by developing new customers and new knowledges.

It is most unlikely that a qualitative business transformation will occur within the framework of the current knowledge and business core. As cited earlier, the defenders of the steady state will resist ideas aimed at making obsolete the present business. Because new ideas rarely make sense and are easy to shoot down, those who resist change have powerful advantages. Moreover, new ideas are peculiar in that it is not

Approaches to Entrepreneurial Strategies

known which among the many will produce positive results. In biology only one frog emerges from a thousand eggs; the same analogy is relevant with business ideas. Despite all these and many other restraints, the business needs an atmosphere of encouraging innovation if transformation is to take place.

A new business, which originates when somebody anticipating a need in society and converting that need into an economic opportunity by investing resources, has no choice but to be entrepreneurially minded. Every new business starts small; it is so busy struggling to survive that motivation for economic achievement permeates the organization. The contention is not that most smaller businesses perform the entrepreneurial function better than large businesses. Statistics argue otherwise. It is that the constant struggle for economic survival dictates an aura of continual entrepreneurial thinking.

For a number of reasons it is difficult to sustain this entrepreneurial spirit in a large organization. Large corporations have a proclivity to think big, often ignoring the reality that everything new starts small. This partially explains why most of the major innovations in the past generation (motels, frozen foods, instant photography, xerography, containerization, the basic oxygen steel furnace, discount houses, franchising, etc.) all emerged from small businesses. Big business has many strengths, but successful innovation has not been a major one.[18]

In focusing simultaneously on the transitional and transformational dimensions of managing change, the Xerox Corporation may prove an exception to the rule of big corporations not distinguishing themselves at innovation. Conducting its research on a two dimensional level, the company's research laboratories in Rochester, New York, are concerned chiefly with the improvement of its current line of products. At the very same time, those in Palo Alto, California, assuming the future obsolescence of paper communication, is concentrating on new and different methods of eliminating the medium of paper in communications.

The budgetary, perceptual and personal attitudes required for innovation are not congenial to the steady state large business. In the traditional and transitional phases of the business, the emphasis is on operating and adapting. The entrepreneur is endeavoring to introduce something novel to transform the business in the long run; whereas, the operating manager is trying to achieve economic performance for today. Both tasks are important, but they are different. The operating manager is always raising the question of whether the cost is necessary, and if it does not produce immediate economic results it is *ipso facto* considered unnecessary. On the other hand, the innovating entrepreneur is always concerned with the question of whether the business is focusing on the right opportunity. It is important for the operating manager to be administratively on top of his job, but this commitment makes it almost impossible to see the business in a new way.

New products are like babies requiring special attention. Their growth is best achieved, at least in their early stages, by being taken care of separately. Successful experiences with innovation by such firms as Minnesota Mining and Manufacturing Corporation and General Electric Company support the contention that it is wise to structure the genuinely new autonomously. The new venture approach has the advantage of combining the entrepreneurial spirit of the small firm with massive resources of the large corporation.

With few exceptions, most of today's big business technology is an outgrowth of the golden age of the American entrepreneur in the late nineteenth century. Such major industries in the United States as automobile, steel, and aluminum will continue to play an important role for the nation's prosperity, but it is doubtful that they will contribute to qualitative economic growth. Big business has been so busy doing what is already known that it has neglected innovation. The "research and development" budget for the genuinely new has been neglected while the major proportion of it has been devoted to adaptation and improvement. The automobile industry is a case in point. During the early years of General Motors Corporation, Charles Kettering, vice-president and general manager of research, operating with a paltry research and development budget, was able to introduce such major breakthroughs as ethyl antiknock gasoline, the self-starter, automotive lighting, crankcase ventilation, the electric frigidaire, and a pioneering Diesel engine. In the past three decades the research and development results, in spite of huge budgetary outlays, have been largely cosmetic, centering on style, comfort and status. In most of the mature established industries, a similar situation of large research expenditures and small results has been the pattern.

Although there is little question that business innovation is far ahead of the public sector, the performance record of big business in creating new knowledge industries has been far from distinguished in terms of cost-benefit ratios. In view of the research allocation toward improving the traditional and adapting in the transitional business, it is hardly surprising, as mentioned earlier, that most of the major innovations in the past generations have emerged from small and medium sized businesses. The next generation will probably witness a reversal of this pattern for two reasons: first, the dwindling importance of the older industries and the rise of new knowledge and system businesses; and, second, society's expectation of change from its powerful institutions. In short, since big business has the talent and the resources, the entrepreneurial task of innovation will receive unprecedented attention and fall increasingly on the shoulders of big business.

American business is slowly discovering the advantages of structuring innovation outside the boundaries of the traditional and transitional dimensions of the business. Minnesota Mining and Manufacturing Corporation, for example, systematically appraises its research and development effort by monitoring carefully the projected expectations of each of its new products. If emulated by other large businesses, the Minnesota Mining and Manufacturing model of entrepreneurship may go down as one of the greatest innovations in American business history. By organizing the transformational business as a separate autonomous function and systematically monitoring research development, managers may prove that the forecasts about the demise of the enterprise system are premature.

THE AMERICAN TELEPHONE AND TELEGRAPH STORY

American Telephone and Telegraph Corporation, one of the most successful companies in business history, provides an excellent clinical case study by its accomplishments in the traditional and transitional phases and the uncertainties it is now facing in shaping its future transformation. Briefly tracing the interaction of all three dimensions in the American Telephone and Telegraph corporate story will help illuminate the strategic flavor of decision making noted in the chapter.

American Telephone and Telegraph, the world's largest privately owned corporation, is a giant among business giants, a supercorporation with nearly a million employees, three million stockholders and approximately ninety billion dollars in capital investment. Along with the ownership of its supply arm, Western Electric Company, the twelfth largest industrial corporation in the United States, it also operates Bell Laboratories, probably the biggest brain factory in the world, with a budget of over $650 million, and with over 2000 employees holding doctorate degrees and with over 3,300 having degrees at the masters level. Company revenues for 1975 were $29.3 billion, with expenses of $26.1 billion and a net income of approximately $3.2 billion. Recitation of additional arresting statistics would only confirm that the Bell System has assembled under private auspices the greatest collection of money, men and material in history.

The formulation of American Telephone and Telegraph's corporate doctrine derives principally from the genius of one man, Theodore Vail, the organizational wizard of communications. In anybody's management's hall of fame list, Vail would have to rank at the top. Without any professional academic discipline to guide him, and often running counter to much of the conventional wisdom of his era, Vail was primarily responsible for making the great qualitative strategic decisions shaping the destiny and establishing the corporate strengths of American Telephone and Telegraph.

In 1908 Vail projected the grand design for the Bell System in the words, "One Policy, One System, Universal Service." In order to achieve this mission a number of other qualitative strategic decisions were necessary. First, he endorsed the principle of regulation at a time when most businessmen considered it an anathema and when both major political parties were urging nationalization of the telephone industry. Second, he introduced the principle of average pricing whereby the heavy users would subsidize in part light users. Third, Vail created a vertically integrated network, recognizing that the telephone had limited utility unless connected to a larger system. Fourth, in order to meet the pressing needs for capital which were limited in a regulated industry, he conceived the startling innovation of democratizing corporate property by creating the middle class investor interested in a stable fixed income for financial security. Fifth, in order to avoid possible government ownership, he committed the company to research which would provide the best service to the customer. Sixth, he rejected the contemporary philosophy of "the public be damned" for the policy of cultivating the public. For Vail, this meant more than public relations rhetoric. He insisted on corporate integrity and on scrupulously honest reporting. In Vail's words: "No, we will lay our cards on the table. There is never anything to be gained by concealment." The essence of Vail's doctrine was later ratified by Congress with the Communications Act of 1934, which stated, ". . . to make available, so far as possible to all the people of the United States, a rapid, efficient, nationwide and worldwide wire and radio communication service with adequate facilities at reasonable cost."

American Telephone and Telegraph Corporation occupies a position of rare distinction in the annals of American business. It is one of the few companies that has fulfilled its original objective. At present ninety-six percent of the population has telephone service, including thirteen percent of the nation's families earning under $5000 a year. In terms of the prohibitive cost involved, complete saturation of the remaining four percent would make little economic sense.

The singular achievement of almost universal service was made possible by two generations of Bell System managers, who, in the transitional stage, converted Vail's original ideas of the business into reality. It is the general consensus that the Bell System provides the most extensive, high quality, economical telecommunication system in the world. American Telephone and Telegraph has an unmatched record in technological excellence. Not only has it pioneered in telephone communications but its research has produced approximately 150 new industries including the laser, the cathode ray tube, the digital computer and the transistor, to cite a few.

Yet, despite its past accomplishments, the future of American Telephone and Telegraph is filled with uncertainty, conflict and controversy. The old Bell System doctrine of corporate identity is being challenged from two major sources—technology and competition. The response to these challenges will determine the future transformation stage of the business.

In a recent past, American Telephone and Telegraph has undermined its old knowledge foundation by shifting from a mechanical or industrial method of communications to an electronic or post-industrial system. Among some of the specific contributions from Bell Laboratories creating a new base of business knowledge are the following: electronic switching stations, pulse code modulation digital computers, optical fibers and light wave transmission, satellite systems, data access devices, mobile telecommunication systems, video phones, and computerized telecommunications.

The impact of the new technology will play an important role in determining what American Telephone and Telegraph's business should be. Once a tidy demarcation was possible between data processing and communications, but with their growing interdependence, the distinction has become blurred. With data communication becoming more and more important, the communication industry is moving in the direction of data processing and the computer industry is shifting closer to communications. For example, International Business Machines Corporation has announced plans for a domestic satellite system for the transmission of data and computer messages between terminal devices and computer centers with the by-passing of the local and toll facilities of the telephone common carriers. Meanwhile, American Telephone and Telegraph is innovating a cathode ray table computer display terminal with data processing capability. With each company fearing encroachment upon its traditional business, it appears that over the next decade International Business Machines and American Telephone and Telegraph will be on a collision course.

The new competition that American Telephone and Telegraph Corporation is currently encountering is the result of recent decisions by the Federal Communications Commission. The most notable of these decisions are: the Carterfone ruling in which it held that American Telephone and Telegraph could not arbitrarily deny the right of customers to hook their own equipment into the Bell System network and the 1971 microwave decision authorizing firms called "specialized common carriers" to compete with American Telephone and Telegraph in providing long distance private line service, i.e., direct lines between two or more points for business customers. These decisions are playing a major role in altering the nature of American Telephone and Telegraph Corporation's business because in the last decade there has been a new infusion of competition in the terminal equipment and private line areas by such new market entrants as terminal equipment manufacturers, large business users seeking to construct their own microwave networks and specialized common carriers. Thus far, the competition has made only miniscule incursions into the vast Bell System market. American Telephone and Telegraph is concerned, however, about future inroads. It argues, moreover, that the competition is "cream skimming" the profits in lucrative markets, ignoring the safety of the network and forcing telephone companies to raise residential rates.

If the future of telecommunications industry is obscure, the strategy stance of American Telephone and Telegraph is not. Over the last decade it has argued that the Federal Communication Commission's enchantment with competition is misguided chiefly because it will produce fragmentation and waste, raise residential prices through cartelized competition as in the case of the railroads, and hinder innovation. AT&T maintains that because it has performed admirably in servicing the country's needs, regulation is still the best way of combining private initiative and the public interest for the communication industry. On the other hand, should competition prevail, the Bell System contends it should be allowed to compete fully in the realm of prices without being constrained by regulatory tariffs.

After failing to convince the Federal Communication Commission of this philosophy over the past decade, American Telephone and Telegraph has now decided to leave the choice of communication policy to the elected representatives rather than the Federal Communications Commission. The result is the proposed Consumer Communication Reform Act in which 200 lawmakers have signed up as co-sponsors. The main provisions of the legislative effort are to stop duplicate competition in long distance services; to revoke the jurisdiction of the Federal Communications Commission over technical and operational standards; to protect the integrity of the network and place them in the hands of the local commissions; to prohibit competitive services by satellite carriers; to allow state utility commission jurisdiction over customer owned equipment; and to permit the telephone companies to use a flexible pricing policy based on "incremental" costs. In short, in terms of what its business should be tomorrow, from American Telephone and Telegraph's perspective, it is to reestablish and revitalize its role as a regulated monopoly according to the present legislation before Congress.

This position is opposed by the Federal Communications Commission which wishes to create a regulated monopoly with competition confined to certain allocated areas, particularly private lines and terminal equipment. The solution proposed by the Justice Department's pending anti-trust suit is that American Telephone and Telegraph should be broken up into a number of discrete segments. On the other hand, certain entrepreneurs would prefer a decrease in regulatory involvement, especially in the area of data processing, and the allowance of true competition to settle the outcome.

These are only a few of the alternatives and questions in the debate revolving around the type of a communications system the nation will adopt. The issue will not be resolved quickly. We can expect the legislative, competitive and regulatory battles will intensify in the coming years. Meanwhile, until the issue is resolved, American Telephone and Telegraph will remain in a state of flux as far as the challenge of transforming its future corporate identity.

CHAPTER IV
Entrepreneurial Tactics

INTRODUCTION

AS THE previous pages have tried to demonstrate, the entrepreneurial task is a dynamic and complex process encompassing three main strategic components: the traditional, which allocates resources for improved performance of the present business; the transitional, which reflects a condition of "becoming" by undertaking new risks and opportunities under conditions of uncertainty; and, the transformational, which deploys resources in the quest of making a new and different business. All three interacting strategies share the entrepreneurial common denominator of shifting resources from less productive to more productive economic results.

Each strategy entails a different degree of uncertainty, ambiguity and disorder, reinforcing the assumption that a totally codified theory of entrepreneurship will always be beyond the grasp of the management practitioner. However, the fact that no completely operational theory exists does not diminish the crucial importance of the task. And unless the task is to surrender to drift, luck and intuition, management has a responsibility to push reason as far as possible by developing a more orderly posture in meeting the challenge.

One such approach in coping with uncertainty is the recognition of past entrepreneurial experience, and from this reality draw upon previous successful practice. The inference is that the business practitioner learns far more from success than failure. Although results will never be guaranteed, a systematic approach has the advantage of having probability work to the advantage of management. Moreover, exploring the pattern of successful business performance will establish the foundation of relevant tactics.

The single most important guideline is the ability of a business to define itself clearly by being aware of its identity, and to become capable of promoting its mission by combining the diversity of its knowledge and marketing components into purposeful unity. Mention has been made earlier of the uniqueness and special excellence of several leading businesses. The brewery, Anheuser-Busch, was singled out on the list of exceptional companies. A more detailed diagnosis of how this particular company defined its identity in responding to the question of "what is our business?" may serve to help explain the decision making process and managerial effectiveness of a major industrial leader.

Anheuser Busch's Answer to "What Is Our Business?"

The beer industry is especially interesting in that it has a homogeneous product with every brewer telling the customer that his beer tastes best. Repeated tests, however, document that only a miniscule minority of consumers can distinguish the taste of one beer from another. Since unique taste is not the answer to economic performance, some other explanation is needed to explain the rationale of consumer choice in selecting one brand of beer over another. Anheuser-Busch, the leader of the brewing industry, is extremely competent in the functional areas of distribution, production, advertising, financing, inventory control, personnel, etc. However, other companies in this homogenous industry can claim similar competencies.

The success of Anheuser-Busch resides less in its functional competencies, important as they are, than in its unique ability to commit itself and develop knowledge in the field of recreation, an area remote from the traditional boundaries of the brewing industry. The slogan "Making Friends Is Our Business" is more than empty public relations rhetoric; the company has tried to make it meaningful by developing family recreation centers on a national scale. Anheuser-Busch has successfully converted its heavy investment in tourist and recreational facilities into a promotional vehicle for marketing and selling its beer. It is not accidental that the company builds its plants adjacent to major tourist attractions such as Colonial Williamsburg; or erects its own recreational facilities in Merrimack, New Hampshire, Grant Farm in Illinois, Houston, Tampa and Los Angeles. When the family visits these tourist attractions during vacations, the imprint of the product is etched clearly in its mind. In addition, it factors into its marketing activities such items as a visit to a brewery on a Gray Line tour, ownership of major league baseball team, or enlisting athletic and theatrical figures for their distributionships. Anheuser-Busch has competency in making beer, but so do others. But only Anheuser-Busch has the ability to interrelate entertainment with its product. After Disneyland, it is first in the country in this field. Diagnosing a business by raising the aforementioned question of knowledge excellence helps determine the objectives, identify the real commitments, and provide a consensus of understanding within the organization. Without a vision of the whole, entrepreneurial tactics will only lead to confusion.

The importance of defining the company's identity in terms of knowledge and marketing cannot be overstated, but it is only the first step in the quest for economic results. Even a business confident of its mission must proceed to make a rigorous analysis of current business activities. Most business plans suffer from the illusion that today's business operations are in good shape. More often than not, a detailed diagnosis of today's business activities indicates that the contrary is true. The deeper the probe into present business activities, the greater the prospect for deciphering misallocation and misdirection of resources. Moreover, it is a truism that what we do today is largely a response to yesterday's circumstances. In taking such decisions for granted there is an inevitable tendency for drift and non-results. Good answers never last forever and always carry with them the law of diminishing returns. The more successful the manager is in eliminating the friction and improving the potential connected with current operations, the greater will be the liberation of energies and resources for new opportunities.

DIAGNOSTIC TOOLS

Unfortunately, codified textbooks with rules and formulae are not issued to managers in coping with the problems of waste and misallocation of resources. Applying entrepreneurial tactics successfully is not teachable, although it may be learnable if the manager thinks through what he is doing in terms of whether or not it makes sense in producing economic results.

In addition to conducting a learning dialogue in the search for improved knowledge from personal experience and studying examples of successful businesses, another available approach in meeting the challenge of systematizing entrepreneurial tactics is the application of diagnostic tools. In essence, diagnosis is the examination of a pattern of uncertainties by formulating hypotheses and then testing these hypotheses within the framework of real situations. At the risk of oversimplification, a business diagnostic configuration has at least three key phases. The first is accepting the reality that many of today's business activities are being performed incompetently, providing, therefore, the opportunity to shift resources from less productive to more productive areas. The second phase is identifying symptoms of misallocation in a particular area in which a modest effort may produce economic dividends. The third is applying the appropriate diagnostic tool to the symptom selected.

The art of diagnosis is not a panacea for problem solving, rather, it is a method of conceptualization enabling management to make sounder business judgments. A word of caution is also in order on the use of the diagnostic tools. In dealing with uncertainty it is not presumed that the proposed diagnostic tools are verities capable of routine and automatic translation. More properly, they should be looked upon as principles, *i.e.*, common denominators found in most business situations. Each of the diagnostic tools to be discussed requires testing for criteria of relevance within the business setting. The key objective of the following pages is to demonstrate how certain diagnostic tools, applied in an entrepreneurial fashion, can make the present business more effective, focus on improved use of physical, human and capital assets, liberate energies away from problems and into opportunities, and create an encouraging atmosphere for managing change. Finally, it is hoped that by exploring the diagnostic tools more concretely, a clearer understanding of their value will emerge for future practice. Specifically, six diagnostic principles will be discussed.

Pareto's Law of Social Distribution

The main distinction between a social principle and physical law is that events falling under the latter are repeatable. Regardless of how many times the physical experiment is conducted under similar circumstances, the result will always be the same. This is the essence of the scientific method. On the other hand, events in the social realm are characterized by irreversibility rather than by repeatability. No amount of social experimentation can convert a man into a boy, a large department store into a country store or a modern steel mill into a blacksmith's shop. However, when it is possible to discern a social pattern based on what we are more or less likely to find in the social universe, and when the social pattern displays a consistent regularity, it is appropriate to call it a principle.

Entrepreneurial Tactics

Vilfredo Pareto's law of social distribution is one such principle useful to managers in diagnosing business patterns of potential misallocation. According to the Italian sociologist and economist, in any configuration of social distribution a small number of elements will be responsible for the preponderant portion of results. In terms of results the vital few within the configuration will always take precedence over the trivial many. To put the principle in an extreme mathematical form, ten percent of the distribution usually accounts for ninety percent of the results; and, vice versa, the remaining ninety percent is responsible for the great bulk of cost and effort.[1]

Pareto's law suggests that most aggregate statistics relating to social situations misrepresent, misdirect and misinform. Activities in any social pattern respond to demands, concealing the ratio between efforts and results. Pareto's law assists management to recognize the inadequacy of information emanating from contrived business composites in the sectors of sales, inventory, costs, revenue and other areas, and helps to focus on those elements producing meaningful results. For example, a common aggregate statistic on mobility is that one out of five people move annually; but, on closer analysis we find that a small number of the same people do most of the moving. Moreover, if one examines the components of aggregate statistics for company products, salesmen's performance, absenteeism, alcoholism, stock ownership, volume of branch banking, and chain stores, etc., he will invariably find that a small number of people or units within the business contribute to the vast majority of results; and, similarly, at the other end of the social spectrum, the majority of people or units account for the overwhelming cost.

Countless specific examples of the Pareto principles abound, but a few representative illustrations will point out its diagnostic relevance in the allocation of business resources.

Lafayette National Bank in Brooklyn announced that it would no longer accept new accounts of under $500 nor pay interest on its old accounts under that figure. The management reasoned that the allocation of resources to these small accounts was a drain on its resources.

The "average" sales manager will spend the vast majority of his time with the ninety percent of the sales force creating most of the costs. His fallacious reasoning is likely to be the top ten percent don't need me, whereas the bottom ninety percent do.

Simple inventory control is another method of stressing the vital few and eliminating the trivial many. Coty, the perfume manufacturer, discovered it could improve its distribution and achieve improved economic results by merging five of its warehouses into one.

In the case of Riunite, the wine company previously mentioned, the vast majority of sales are generated from five products out of hundreds in the company's line.

In making a distinction between the vital few and the trivial many, management can improve its asset management by making its capital work more effectively. For example, American Telephone and Telegraph Corporation discovered that only fifteen percent of its subscribers use information services with any degree of regularity. Meanwhile, the remaining eighty-five percent are supporting, through rate payments, the minority of users. Consequently, many of the operating companies are requesting a change in rates from the local commission to make the heavy user of the information service pay proportionately.

A major exception to Pareto's law, one in which a small number of events do not dictate the mass of results, is difficult to find in any category of social activities. It is not possible to repeal this principle; but, after rigorous analysis, it may be possible to alter the ratios between effort and results. If the manager could change the percentage proportion from ninety-ten, to sixty-forty, seventy-thirty, or even eighty-twenty, misallocation could be reduced and results improved. To be specific, if ten percent of the sales force is contributing ninety percent of the results and the other ninety percent of the sales force is producing most of the cost, then the elimination of marginal performers and improvement of mediocre performers should be a priority commitment. Eliminating non-productive efforts will enhance performance.

The more the Pareto principle is explored, the greater the relevance to managerial work. In exploring the result area of any business, most contributions come from a few employees and few groups. Qualitatively, in any business the entrepreneurial contribution of managing for results makes other jobs possible. Most executives are pushed by the drift of events, allowing little time for real performance. Implementing policies and performing routine tasks are an important part of a manager's job. Neglecting administrative functions can threaten an executive's career. At the same time a common characteristic of outstanding executives is their ability to escape the activity trap of being a prisoner of routine and a captive of time. Despite the pressures they find time for the thinking aspect of their job. The managerial challenge is to find the ten percent disposable time to make a meaningful contribution. The accountant, for example, will spend almost as much time on the first ninety-eight percent of his audit as on the last two percent. In view of this ratio of efforts to results, he would be acting wisely if he accounted for the last two percent randomly. Similarly, when managers become aware of this cost-benefit ratio in the ecology field, the task of convincing conservationists of the need of rational tradeoffs should be easier. At the very least, exploring the relevance of the Pareto principle punctures the illusion of aggregate statistics by forcing the manager to think through what he is doing in terms of efforts and results.

Cost and Revenue Streams—
The Transaction Analysis

In appraising current business performance, the relationship between the cost and revenue streams is a useful financial indicator of resource allocation. In the conventional cost accounting model, the accountant is compelled by tax and government regulations to find a place for everything spent in the budget. For those areas that are less clearcut, he sets up various definitions within the cost structure. The approach is valid for computing direct cost in a business with homogenous product lines. However, the model has little validity for a large company with multi-product lines where often the factor of allocation transcends the legal boundaries of the business.

In such a situation where a product mix exists which is common to most large businesses, the revenue and cost flows do not represent a single money stream; the unitary stream is part of the accountant's model but it is not always the reality of economic results. Recent application of distribution accounting techniques has confirmed the role of product mix contributions in appraising economic results. In utilizing these techniques, the revenue and cost streams are not a closed loop; each must be viewed separately but in relationship to each other. Unlike the narrow accounting definition of cost which concentrates on the inner boundaries of the business, the entrepreneurial definition views cost more broadly, basing it on what the customer actually pays for the product or service. What the customer pays for the product or service is true cost; all the rest is allocation in one form or another. To cite just one example, when the consumer buys a loaf of bread in the supermarket, he is paying for the total spectrum of costs—the farmer, warehouser, baker, the rack jobber, the wholesaler and the retailer. As far as the consumer is concerned, he pays for all phases in the distribution process which cumulatively account for his total cost.

A more realistic method for encompassing the interrelationship between the cost and revenue streams is the application of transaction analysis. This financial principle states that revenue is roughly proportionate to volume and that cost is roughly proportionate to the number of transactions (minus the fixed raw material cost factor). In focusing on transaction analysis it is not only possible to locate the key cost centers within the total range of the cost process; but, in addition, if this is done with each product or service, it becomes possible to determine more accurately the performance among the marginal, mediocre and star performers within the business.[2]

To cite a general illustration, applying the test of the transaction analysis reveals that the general supporting costs of obtaining a large order will be roughly proportionate to those of obtaining a small one. That is, production costs, paper, advertising, promotional and sales effort, etc., will be about the same; however, the volume of revenue from a larger order (with proper deduction for raw material) will be of a higher financial magnitude. Concomitantly, the cost of a product failure or a non-sale is roughly the same as the economic successes. Similarly, in the pursuit of innovation the administrative and supporting costs of a product failure will be of the same magnitude as successes, except that the former do not find their way into the revenue streams. At the same time the allocations for failure must be made by the accountant in the budget and this depends on his definitions; however, when it is done on an aggregate basis of unifying the cost and revenue streams there is a tendency to confuse the pattern of economic results within the business. On the other hand, transaction analysis in viewing them as a separate but interrelated stream helps identify the real economic costs and contributions.

The initial advantage of the early discounters over the department stores is a specific example of the transaction analysis in practice. The traditional merchandising rationale of the department store was "thick on the best, thin on the rest" for its product line, whereas the discounters operated on the theory of "thick on the best, the hell with the rest." Instead of pursuing the department store philosophy of favoring a conventional percentage markup or profit margin, the discounters focused on the entire revenue stream by concentrating on those items which had a more rapid turnover and greater cash flow. Unlike most traditional department stores which carried countless categories of products, Sears Roebuck and Company has always recognized the distinction between cost and revenue by carrying only three types of basic products—good, better and best. In short, Sears was practicing the alleged innovation of the discounters long before it came on the scene.

A close conceptual affinity exists between the Pareto principle and transactional analysis. For example, the success stories of the Seven-

Entrepreneurial Tactics

Eleven and other convenience grocery stores across the country were based on the application of these diagnostic tools. A typical supermarket has over 10,000 items, but only a small percentage of these products contribute significantly to economic results. The entrepreneurs of the small grocery variety stores selected only the top 200 or so revenue producing items. As a result they were able to build lucrative businesses with a percentage of profit on sales far exceeding the average supermarket.

In terms of costs and results the sales function is an area of frequent misallocation, but it is also an area of opportunity for human resource management. Many corporations spend a great deal of money on sales training. Yet, regardless of the scope and rigor of the program, results are bound to be marginal because sales training alone is not the critical factor contributing to a salesman's performance. Perhaps the single most important common denominator in producing results for most sales forces hinges on the number of calls made by each salesman. The importance of sales visits also vividly points out that the single most important asset of a salesman is time. Unfortunately, an examination of a salesman's time often reveals a disproportionate amount of activity to non-selling functions such as traveling, filling out forms, setting up appointments, and other mundane jobs. Because sales training will only result in marginal improvement among individual salesmen, the insight of the trivial many versus the vital few should alert management that the key factor is the removal of the restraints by a more systematic management of time. One company overcame one of these obstacles by hiring high school girls on a part-time basis to do the salesman's paperwork thereby enabling him to allot more time to calling on customers.

In most businesses the annual cost reduction program is as predictable as April showers. But such a control device, in making cuts across the board without regard to performance, is seriously deficient. Costs never exist by themselves, for no matter how cheap or efficient the effort is, it is waste if it is devoid of results. Focusing on results through transactional analysis is the best and most effective cost control. In staff work, for example, increasing the size of the budget is frequently the main objective, whether or not economic results are forthcoming. More often than not there is a low correlation between large staff budgets and economic results.

Transaction analysis is a useful diagnostic tool providing a form of feedback whereby support costs are geared to economic contributions. Controlling the product mix through transactional analysis enables the firm to sell a larger proportion of product breadwinners and deploy fewer resources to low turnover items, thereby improving turnover of capital and cash flow.

The Mirage of Planned Obsolescence

Another deterrent operating against entrepreneurial effectiveness and contributing to misdirection of resources is the tendency of many businesses to resist change. When one looks closely at the American business environment, the much publicized concept of planned obsolescence is often more of a mirage than a reality. Adherence to steady state activities and practices based on yesterday's decisions inhibits innovation and defends the past. More concretely, the problem of managing change systematically becomes more onerous when the functional perceptions of employees take precedence over the customer's view of value. Among the most prominent examples of specialized laser beam vision obstructing change and reinforcing the equilibrium of the stationary state are the following: the technologists' perception of utility, meaningless product variety, the pseudo-arguments of specialists and managerial ego.

Limitations of Technological Vision

The parochial mentality fostered by many engineers and scientists in pushing the esoteric product approach helps explain the gap between research and development allocation and the slim results in many businesses. Building a better mousetrap is no guarantee that the consumer will beat a path to the door. Sophisticated and ingenious design is worthless if isolated from the consumer's value system; no value exists unless the customer is willing to pay for it.

The technological focus has many strengths, but its uncritical application can be dangerous. Stripped of all its esoteric vocabulary, the engineer's definition of value and utility stresses durability, expensive material, inordinate precision and design for perpetuity. Satisfaction for the engineer too often resides in the intellectual challenge of the task, the amount of difficulty in overcoming the challenge and the degree of approbation from his colleagues in the profession. Many scientists also have a strong inclination for accomplishing what is interesting, ignoring the factor of economic results. Lacking any real reference point of consumer satisfaction, this monistic technological approach is irrelevant and rarely contributes anything toward business results. Although the product may receive professional endorsement in the learned journals, the over-engineered product with inane quality standards is an incubus if it does not make a value-added contribution to the customer.

American industry lost a large share of the turbine market because it designed them for perpetuity. The added effort and deep thinking that went into the over-engineered turbines as part of that cost were immaterial to the consumer. Many other examples mirror the tunnel vision of corporate technicians—two famous ones come immediately to mind. The General Electric Company and the RCA Corporation pushed their research efforts to improve the qualities of the vacuum tube. Meanwhile, the American Telephone and Telegraph Corporation invented the transistor; but, it was the small unknown Texas Instrument Company and a new crop of Japanese entrepreneurs operating initially in garages who successfully marketed it and assured the obsolescence of the vacuum tube. Engineers in the typewriter industry concentrated their energies in the direction of producing more carbon copies, ignoring the reality of xerography. Superfluous engineering emphasis misdirects energies, ties up physical and human resources and acts as a restraint on innovation.

In the examples cited, it would be unfair to assign complete blame on the scientists and the engineers. In most instances they received their orders from top management. The real fault was in the failure by management to see the business in terms of customer needs. Raw materials and technological processes are of no concern to the consumer. He is only concerned with utility or what the product can do for him. By focusing narrowly on their internal technology, these managements failed to perceive that other alternatives existed for satisfying customer needs.

Meaningless Product Variety

Meaningless variety, the proclivity to provide frills and extraneous extras which are divorced from the customer value system, is another negative factor inhibiting growth. Any company maintaining inventory for thousands of grades and variations of a product is essentially useless if the customer cannot tell the difference. The number of combinations and permutations for colors in the paint industry is almost infinite. A brief look at the endless varieties of just the color "blue" in a paint company's catalogue reveal countless choices, including such esoteric variations as: robin's egg, sky, baby, electric, as well as others. The question arises as to what extent the variety is simply cosmetic and to what degree the list contributes to customer value and economic results? Meaningful variety is another matter. In this instance, since the customer is willing to pay, it is not really cost-added but value-added in a true sense.

*Dangers of Specialists Without a Total
View of the Business*

The pseudo-arguments of professional specialists within the business are additional manifestations of the diminution of obsolescence and the stifling of opportunity. Frequently, tax and financial people in the organization argue for the continuation of a burdensome mediocre product because it absorbs overhead. Such financial gimmickry is deceptive. If the product contributes nothing toward economic results, it is surreptitiously pirating precious resources away from opportunities. Without tangible and documentary evidence, this is a variation of the fallacy that "two can live as cheaply as one."

A similar shibboleth is the salesman's credo of needing a "full product line," an argument which is frequently more emotional than entrepreneurial. Entrepreneurial thinking demands that the burden of economic argument rests upon those who argue for a full product line. Without economic justification, the argument is a genuflection to the status quo and is another example of feeding problems and starving opportunities. The pseudo-arguments of specialists have the enervating and dangerous impact of allowing functional experts to make fragmented entrepreneurial decisions without understanding their nature or impact. The contribution of professional specialists is important; but specialists who lack a vision of the total business are liabilities rather than assets to the entrepreneurial function.

Managerial Ego

Finally, managerial ego is another hindrance to obsolescence. This is a human, but entrepreneurially unsound characteristic of placing excessive reliability on individual or group infallibility. Managerial ego tends to support projects in terms of money, talent and resources in order to prove that the initial managerial commitment was correct. Business history is strewn with cases of management refusing to own up to mistakes and attempting to camouflage them with increased budgetary allocations. The result is a form of creative accounting which is at best a self-fulfilling prophecy attempting to manipulate expectations which more often than not defy probability. The prospects of success diminish the more one tries to substitute the hubris of managerial ego in trying to prove a point which runs counter to the reality of economic performance.

All of the above-mentioned fallacies rarely contribute to obsolescence, but more important they rigidify change by adding flaccid figments to the ghost of yesterday's business instead of providing needed muscle for the innovation of tomorrow, which should be the major concern of entrepreneurial thinking.

Abandonment

All the previously mentioned diagnostic tools point to the concept of abandonment. Recognition of this concept is probably the single most important tactical guideline in the quest for economic results. If there is any real key in the management of change, it is the ability to jettison marginal products and non-productive activities. Attempts to resurrect the efficiency of marginal products can at best result in improvement, and are usually a waste of time, talent and money. A sounder assumption is to accept the fact that whatever exists is getting old and that the forces of competition will in time obsolete the product. Often it is entrepreneurially sounder for the company to obsolete a marginal product before the competition; there is nothing wrong with committing product euthanasia and removing it from the business. Rather than postpone the inevitable end of a product which has passed its economic zenith by applying the elixirs of sales promotion, advertising, and defensive research, the best therapy for the business from the point of view of total business performance is to purge itself of marginal mediocrities.

Weeding out the product garden is as important in the business as it is on the farm. One sobering method of avoiding the false therapy of putting too much effort into the soil bed of yesterday's products is to raise the pragmatic question, "If we were not presently in this product or service would we risk going into it today?" The old cow requires the same amount of food as the young one, but she does not produce nearly the same amount of milk. The conclusion is clear that the business should starve its problems but feed its opportunities. As a simple rule of thumb no business can have enough effective things going for it, but with ineffective things the less of them the better. The worst sin a company can practice is to do a little bit more efficiently what should not be done at all. The inclination not to give anything up is the main culprit in reinforcing the steady state mentality and inhibiting change. Most successful companies work systematically on abandonment procedures, but they are the exception rather than the rule. As an example, Hunt Wesson Foods, a subsidiary of Norton Simon Inc., cut its product line from thirty to three during an eleven year period, yet increased sales from $15 million to $120 million.[3]

However, if the principle of abandonment is so self-evident then why is its application the exception more than rule? High on the list of operating realities restricting abandonment are the familiarity with and sentimentality for old products, the apologia that the old product has been good to us as a past profit maker, the energy and effort already invested by many groups within the organization, the personal commitment of top management, and the fear that new products will disturb the familiarity of current operations. These are but a few of the excuses for failure to abandon. Although an outsider with a detached view knows less about the business operations, he is often able to recognize them as alibis for continuing to support the steady state. Since he is not part of the establishment, the outside observer frequently can see the need for abandonment more clearly than the people inside the organization who are prisoners of an internal perception.

Failure to abandon marginal stores largely accounted for the demise of the W. T. Grant Company and the near debacle of the Great Atlantic and Pacific Tea Company. On the other hand, a principal reason for the outstanding retailing performance of Kresge's K-Mart stores over the past decade was its ability to jettison its mediocre performing outlets in the central cities and to establish compact frilless discount stores attracting middle class customers in the new suburban shopping centers.

In dealing with the principle of abandonment, a final word of caution is in order. When businessmen hear the term abandonment they sometimes apply it with the same degree of intensity with people as with products, frequently using it as an excuse to get rid of people they dislike. As a general rule on abandonment, products should be treated ruthlessly; but, with people, loyalty and conscience should be factored into the decision.

Testing New Endeavors

Daniel Bernouilli's theorem, the insight of an eighteenth century statistician, provides an interesting potential application for product abandonment. Briefly, the theorem infers that in any new series of social endeavors, the probability of achieving successful performance is reduced fifty percent with each succeeding effort.[4] The proclivity to combat probability by persevering until the bitter end may be emotionally tempting, but it is almost never entrepreneurially sound. According to the premise of the Bernouilli theorem, a more pragmatic approach in evaluating new company products would be to launch two or three all-out endeavors, and if there are still no economic results then admit that the economic wisdom of abandonment should prevail over managerial tenacity. The old slogan that if at first you do not succeed then try, try again may have relevance in certain situations; but entrepreneurially, it makes more sense to try once or twice, perhaps three times at the most, and then forget about it.

In the practice of medicine, the application of the Bernouilli theorem is the unwritten credo of good diagnosticians. For instance, after several unsuccessful attempts at discovering the patient's ailment, a competent diagnostician will cease further efforts and will pass the case on to somebody else who can bring a fresh perception to the problem. The clinical case histories of the DeSoto and the Edsel in the automotive industry perhaps best reflect the insight of the Bernouilli theorem. Both cars were monumental failures, but the long term effort over several decades to resuscitate the DeSoto was the more disastrous of the two. The Edsel was quickly eliminated by Ford, but misguided efforts to convert the DeSoto from a marginal performer to an economic breadwinner lasted close to a generation and almost destroyed the Chrysler Corporation.

The normal operating practices of the publishing and food manufacturing industries foster an inbuilt automatic abandonment pattern. In their quest for a best seller, publishers are aware of the futility of combating probability. As a general rule if a book fails to achieve best seller status in three months, even the most vigorous promotion campaigns are of little avail. Similarly, in the case of food manufacturers, if a new product is not successful within a six to eight week period it will be automatically removed from the shelf by the supermarket manager.

Finally, as discussed in previous pages, the great advantage of the market system is not the function of profit but the function of loss, which factors abandonment of unsuccessful products out of the system. Non-market systems, such as governments, can provide goods and services but they lack an objective standard for eliminating obsolete products and services.

Concentration

Closely allied with the principle of abandonment is the corollary concept of concentration or the principle of least effort, never using more premises than are actually needed. The principle known as Occam's Razor was first systematically advanced by the medieval Franciscan philosopher, William of Occam. It states that it is vain to do with more what can be done with fewer.[5] For centuries medical and scientific research, in attempting to separate the relevant from the irrelevant, has successfully applied a variation of the Occam principle called the "law of scientific parsimony." If you have one explanation for a phenomenon then there is no need to seek a second explanation.

The ability of management to concentrate (of never using more premises than are actually needed) on its knowledge excellences is the single most important common denominator for all successful businesses. Although a company may do many things competently, the odds are against a company doing a myriad of things brilliantly. The recent poor performance of most conglomerates confirms this business axiom. Operationally, concentration is synonymous with the concept of setting and focusing organizational effort on a few basic opportunities. Companies such as Midas (mufflers), Rayco (seatcovers), Lee Myles (transmissions) and Drago (shoe repairs) reflect this ability to concentrate by combining skilled people and appropriate tools in offering a specialized approach to service.

These key opportunity priorities should hinge on the recognized strengths of the company. Clear objectives are also of crucial importance in providing an entrepreneurial screen to filter the relevant from the irrelevant. In short, if the project does not fit the company's knowledge excellence and marketing competence, the danger exists that the risk may dilute company strengths. Moreover, in establishing a list of priorities based on perceived opportunities in the marketplace, the least of management's problems is obtaining a sufficient number of new ideas. Invariably there are more ideas than there are available resources. Determining which ideas to start with and which to eliminate inevitably produce the friction in planning among executives. The result is usually an effort at consensus which is the antithesis of concentration.

On pages forty-eight through fifty, a number of instances were cited indicating how successful companies concentrated on their special knowledge excellences. The case of Music Corporation of America (MCA) is additional vivid proof of a company which by concentrating on its mission was able to convert entrepreneurial opportunities into astonishing results. Today it dominates the television and motion picture industry, providing one-quarter of the prime time television shows and launching a number of outstanding financial movie success stories as *The Sting, American Graffiti* and *Jaws* (the latter in grossing $187 million has become the second greatest money maker of all time).

MCA owes its success primarily to Lew Wasserman's sharply focused vision of marrying television and the movies. A·former talent agent, Wasserman in 1940 owned one of the two television sets in California. At a time when most people considered it a toy, he saw it as an instrument which would revolutionize the entertainment industry. After World War II, when television made its entry into American homes, the movie moguls arrogantly ignored it, insisting they were in the movie business and not the broad based entertainment business. Meanwhile, as the booming sale of television sets eroded the movie market, the cinema palaces were converted into bingo parlors and supermarkets while the old studio lots were sold to real estate developers. Wasserman saw his opportunity for the future blending of television and movies with the purchase of Universal Studios' decrepit movie lot. Initially he proceeded to produce pilots for the networks, innovating the sixty and later ninety minute drama programs for prime time.

With a tenacity of purpose and a singular all consuming energy, his next step was the introduction of "world premiere" movies, especially adapted for television. This innovation enabled him to spread overhead costs over a twelve month period, instead of the normal eight month cycle used by other television producers. Moreover, he also sold his world premiere features as pilots for new television series, which, in effect, meant he was selling his own knowledge over and over again. In combining the movies with television he produced such commercial successes as: *Columbo, The Rockford Files, Emergency* and *McCloud*. Next, using the same strategy, Wasserman pioneered the serialization of novels with such successful projects as *Rich Man, Poor Man* and *Captains and Kings*.

Refusing vacations and abjuring hobbies, he also produced additional economic dividends through the rerun syndication of his projects in the domestic and international market. Finally, he introduced a host of incremental, but lucrative tie-in projects such as studio tours, "Kojak" lollipops, "Emergency" lunch boxes, "Bionic" dolls and "Jaws" T-shirts. His accomplishments, as a result of concentrating on the marriage of television and movies, are particularly impressive for an industry which is considered the riskiest in American business. Wasserman refuses to rest on his past laurels; he is concentrating on tomorrow. Believing that video disc entertainment has unlimited potential, he is currently engaged in a joint venture arrangement with N. V. Philips' Gloeilampenfabrieken, the Dutch electronic giant.[6]

In the previous chapter on strategic policies, the importance of determining what is not our business was noted. The concept merits equal emphasis in tactical thinking. In following the principle of least effort, it is important to determine the posteriorities, or what do we leave out. The secret of concentration is to learn how to be paid over and over again for the same business knowledge while avoiding the temptation to compromise and do a little bit of everything. Since resources are limited, the fewer the number on which they can be concentrated the better, providing of course they are allocated to real opportunities. Consequently, setting priorities is the easiest part of the entrepreneurial job, more important is the factor of posteriorities, that is, what projects do we refuse to flirt with despite their alluring temptations. The posteriority area takes on critical significance in identifying the area of concentration on those few projects to which we are genuinely committed for economic results.

Vulnerability Analysis

The diagnostic tool of vulnerability analysis provides still another method for identifying misallocation and possibly stimulating entrepreneurial change. Drawn from the vocabulary of "general systems theory," vulnerability connotes that within any system there will always be sensitive areas, *i.e.*, those points carrying the peak load and on which the greatest pressure on the system is exerted. All open systems have vulnerabilities; and business enterprise is no exception.

Because any business always pays disproportionately for the peak loads the system must bear, searching out the vulnerable pressure points enables management to understand the threats to the enterprise. Any business which has a high break-even point in terms of volume (necessity to run at about ninety-eight percent capacity to make a profit) and a high break-even point in terms of price is highly vulnerable. The paper and steel industries fit this pattern and are ready for major breakthroughs from a technological point of view.[7] Equally important, in seeking out the areas in which the system is operating below standards, management, in identifying the weakest points in the system, may be able to convert vulnerabilities into economic opportunities.

Identifying the major area of vulnerability is a judgmental act, and consequently, it may be subject to different interpretations. However, through dialogue and discussion it is probable that management can arrive at a general consensus. For example, in a cursory examination of several selected industries, there would probably be general agreement on the major vulnerability and the place where commitment of present resources may produce greater economic results. In the steel industry the major pressure point is the factor of heat; the process requires continuous cooling and quenching. The oxygen air blast furnace was a major breakthrough attacking the vulnerability. The major cost in transportation is the carrier at rest. Research devoted to improving the speed of the airplane, bus, truck, railroad and ship was misdirected and provided only marginal results. When marine shipping attacked the vulnerability of the carrier at rest through containerization, it was able to reduce port time from twelve days to twelve hours, resulting in major economic benefits.

Theodore Levitt, Professor of Business Administration at Harvard University, cites: "Development of unit trains and integral trains that carry over long distances, only a single commodity (e.g., coal by the Baltimore and Ohio Railroad, grain by the Illinois Central with few or no intermediate steps. By providing fast long trains at enormous efficiency, the train can dead-head back and still save money. In the case of B and O, its original unit train reduced the round trip time between the West Virginia coal fields and Baltimore from 21 to 7 days."[8] In the lumber industry the business traditionally paid for the whole tree, but obtained economic results from only about twenty-five percent. Successful companies in this industry have been able to convert the former waste (saw dust, leaves, bark, and roots) into new products. In the film processing cycle there are various stages of handling, starting with the customer, to the retailer, and on to the company lab. In attacking the vulnerability, the Polaroid Land camera eliminated these cumbersome steps by producing a picture that developed almost immediately. Shelf space is the critical factor for food, soft drink, beer and biscuit manufacturers; if they failed to get this crucial shelf space they would be stuck with massive inventories. Through a variety of methods, various companies have been able to convert the problem into economic results. For a sales force the key vulnerability is time. If a salesman spends excessive time with paper work and travel, he cannot produce results. Again, companies which have been able to modify these pressures by allowing the salesman to sell have been most successful.

Perhaps the feasibility of vulnerability analysis will be clearer if we try to apply it in greater detail to the supermarket industry. If we assume that tomorrow will be different, then we can conclude that the supermarket of today will not be the same three to five years hence. Looking at the supermarket as a system reveals that its major vulnerability is the checkout counter. This is the pivotal point contributing to sub-par performance and becomes a potential portent for a change within the entire system. From a logical viewpoint the checkout counter makes little sense, since it is a major bottleneck producing friction in the distribution flow throughout the entire system. In the present supermarket pattern, the customer selects his choices from thousands of products and places them in a shopping cart, stands in a long line at the checkout point, removes the articles on a tray for pricing, exchanges money to complete the transaction, packages the goods in shopping bags, and puts them back into the cart only to remove them into a car. A systems analyst would argue that improved technology could eliminate many of these cumbersome stages by eliminating the checkout counter. Moreover, throughout the system there are unskilled clerks doing the manual work of labeling and shelving; union demands are escalating costs; consumers are confused in selecting among eight to ten thousand items; traffic jams choke up the aisles; and pilferage is increasingly common.

It is reasonable to assume that because of the pressures in the system, a new type of supermarket will emerge in the near future. The precise type of retail outlet of the future is still anybody's guess. The new "Seven-Eleven" shops are already one example; they reflect an enactment of Pareto's law in concentrating on a handful of rapid turnover items. The electronic sensing scanner, a celebrated innovation to record prices more rapidly at the checkout counter, is now in operation in several chains. It is too early to determine its performance, but it is doubtful that it will radically improve the system. Given the nature of the vulnerability, perhaps the focus should be in eliminating the checkout counter altogether. With the low profit margins in the industry of less than one percent, it is unlikely that a major innovation will come from within. It is probable that, because of their superior technological competence, the real breakthrough will come from a large data processing company or a major bank. Many different prototypes (video shopping, mobile stores, computer-type stores, cashless stores) are already in the pilot stage. Perhaps none of these innovations will be successful, and maybe on the retail horizon somebody is working on a completely new form of supermarket.

Predicting the future of the supermarket is a hazardous task because of the emerging reality of a cashless society. Innovations in the computer and microcircuitry field are paving the way for electronic funds transfer which will ultimately replace money and checks as the medium of exchange. Because of the inbuilt traffic advantages, more housewives are presently cashing checks in supermarkets than in banks. In several states plans are underway to convert supermarkets into branch banks. Whether the courts will give final approval is still a matter of conjecture. In any event the informational revolution is already altering the work force of the supermarket. Retailing is one of the last bastions of unskilled labor in the economy. The supermarket, however, as a result of technological innovations is adding more and more knowledge workers. The only thing we know for certain is that the structural supermarket of today will probably not be around a decade from now.

MARKETING AND MANAGERIAL GUIDELINES

Impressive intellectual achievements have been made over the past generation in the academic fields of marketing and management. In addition to improved techniques in market research, distribution, advertising, human relations, sales training and management science, the overall conceptual foundations of both disciplines have benefited from the systems approach. Although the uncertainty associated with the fields preclude scientific accuracy, it is reasonable to conclude that the business practitioner of today has substantial conceptual advantages over his counterpart a generation ago. Both disciplines have the advantage of seeing the business as a totality. Once the customer and knowledge are viewed as the center of the business, a fragmented approach becomes unfeasible. This pattern of interdependence is the real meaning of the marketing approach and the managerial systems concept.

The Competitive Environment

The element of competition is an inescapable feature of a business society in the throes of change. As cited earlier, even American Telephone and Telegraph, the mightiest titan in the business world with over $90 billion in assets, is not immune from the competitive winds of change. As a result of recent regulatory decisions, the company has been forced to undergo an identity crisis away from its traditional monopolistic stance and toward a more competitive mode. The chief reason for the transition has been the steady eroding of the company's knowledge foundation. The revolutionary impact of the transistor and recent electronic innovations in microcircuitry, many of which emerged from "Ma Bell's cookbook," have spawned a host of entrepreneurs who are introducing new products and services to meet the communications needs of society.

Although competition is an economic imperative for any business, its relevance in entrepreneurial thinking does not rest on slavish imitation.

According to social scientist, Lewis Mumford, the mechanical timepiece is one of the oldest and most permanent of western civilization's contributions to technology.[9] The fact that it dates back to the late Middle Ages probably explains why modern watch manufacturers failed to visualize alternative methods for telling time. Moreover, the watch industry viewed competition as confined exclusively among the participants in its own industry.

Consequently, the Bulova Watch Company and other leading watch manufacturers ignored the potential threat to their survival emanating from their non-competitors. Meanwhile, a number of electronic firms, most notably, Texas Instruments and Fairchild, were applying their knowledge of micro-circuitry to the production of digital watches. The electronic firms have already made heavy inroads, contending within a decade that mechanical watches will undergo the fate of buggy whips. In terms of business competition, the conclusion is that management, of course, must continually maintain sensing mechanisms to monitor the competition; but, often more crucial to the survival of an industry is the activity of the non-competition.

Although business reality dictates the use of a sensing mechanism to screen what others in the same industry are doing, the tactical key in seeking opportunity areas is to determine what the competition is not doing. Adaptation to what everybody else is doing is almost always the wrong entrepreneurial approach; in all probability, the results will be marginal. The old aphorism of catching the big fish in the spot where everybody else is fishing applies to the realm of business competition. Edwin H. Land, the inventor of the Land camera and founder of the Polaroid Corporation, embraced a singular entrepreneurial view of competition, when he stated: "We never had any competition. Our competition is our own sense of excellence. We are alone because at each stage of invention if what we plan is ten times harder than anybody else can do and twice as hard as we can do."[10]

Imitating such successes as International Business Machines, Sears Roebuck, DuPont, General Electric, or other companies defeats the possibility of achieving a leadership position. Recognition that there is always more than one way of developing a mass market makes more sense than following the leader. When the government forced the Aluminum Corporation of America to give up its virtual monopolistic position, Kaiser Industries, Reynolds Metals Company and other aluminum companies proved there were numerous ways of meeting the customer's needs by enlarging the vision of the market.

Economic results are earned by entrepreneurial leadership, the ability to do something distinctive, not by simply reflecting the competence of others. Moreover, size *per se*, does not assure brilliant economic performance. If this were the case then United States Steel Corporation would excel as an economic performer. Profits, the measurement of economic results, is one of the rewards for innovation and distinctive contribution. The bandwagon philosophy of adaptation fails to meet this test. If the opportunity is real, the only place for the entrepreneur is at the head of the parade. All the clinical evidence indicates that it takes just as much effort, but of a different kind, to be a mediocre performer as it does to be a successful one. The ratio of efforts to results also applies to failure as it does for leadership. The case of General Motors and Studebaker is only one of many examples.

The Pepsi Cola Story

One successful illustration of focusing on what the competition is not doing took place in the soft drink industry. Twenty years ago, the Coca Cola Company, a national institution in its own right, had almost seventy-five percent of market share, the Pepsi Cola Company limped along as a poor second with about fifteen percent, and the rest of the industry accounted for the remainder. At the time the Pepsi bottling franchises were the lowest priced in the soft drink market.

When Albert Steele assumed control of the Pepsi Cola Bottling Company in the early nineteen fifties, he made a strategic decision not to take on Coca Cola in its areas of strength, specifically, fountain sales, the established geographic markets and the older generation. In making his entrepreneurial commitments, he resolved to concentrate in other areas and build up his own excellences. He abandoned the old depression slogan which built the company of "twice as much for a nickel too" and successfully identified and appealed specifically to the youth market. The image of Pepsi Cola soon became the symbol of the youth generation. Steele also selected twenty-six prime marketing targets, most notably in the growing Southwest (Dallas, Phoenix, Tucson, Los Angeles, Forth Worth, Houston, Las Vegas) for his major promotional thrust. Finally, he concentrated his marketing efforts on the supermarket, the ghettos of the central city, and the international market which were increasing in importance. As a result of these key commitments, he created a host of millionaire franchisers and elevated Pepsi Cola's share of market to over thirty percent of a much larger market. Steele could not accomplish this by having Pepsi Cola copy the leader. He aspired to make it a leader.

Finally, the company that only imitates in its corporate strategy of survival faces the danger of being overwhelmed by the novel and unexpected. Without the habit of thinking through and maximizing opportunity, without the practice of coping with the unknown and uncertain, without the experience of failure in encountering tomorrow, a company becomes, by stealth, a prisoner of frozen rigidity, making it vulnerable in an economy of radical change. Putting resources into what has already happened is a timing risk, and is usually against the imitator who finds it is too late and opportunity has passed him by. When detergents emerged on the market, the Fels Company, a leading soap manufacturer, refused to make a commitment, maintaining that detergents were not good enough yet. Commitment to the new is not possible by imitation, nor is it possible to attain from books or vicarious experience of consultants; it is only feasible through diligent application. Dynamic competition makes it inescapable that a company nourish an entrepreneurial spirit by devoting some portion of its resources in going beyond the stable state of defending yesterday.

Life Cycle Analysis

The life cycle model which assumes that individual products undergo a pattern of growth and decay similar to biological organisms is another analytical tool assisting in the management of change. It advances the notion that for most products there is a life span capable of separation into several distinct phases. The typical life cycle pattern includes the following stages: incubation, development, growth, maturity and decline.[11]

Because no two products will have the same duration, management must make a judgment about the product's total projected longevity and the approximate length of its various stages. Careful attention to a product's life span enables management to obtain a clearer allocation of the product's cost allocation and contribution to economic results in all phases of its existence. For example, the spectrum of life cycles ranges from the apparently endless longevity of the aspirin to fad products lasting a few months. In between the two extremes are numerous estimated life cycles. Also, within the various stages, there will often be wide areas of judgment and interpretation regarding the time duration of each stage. The important point, however, is the recognition that no product's life span is eternal and that commitment and resources should only be properly allocated over its calculated longevity.

Graphically, the life cycle product curve assumes the following shape:

Entrepreneurial Tactics

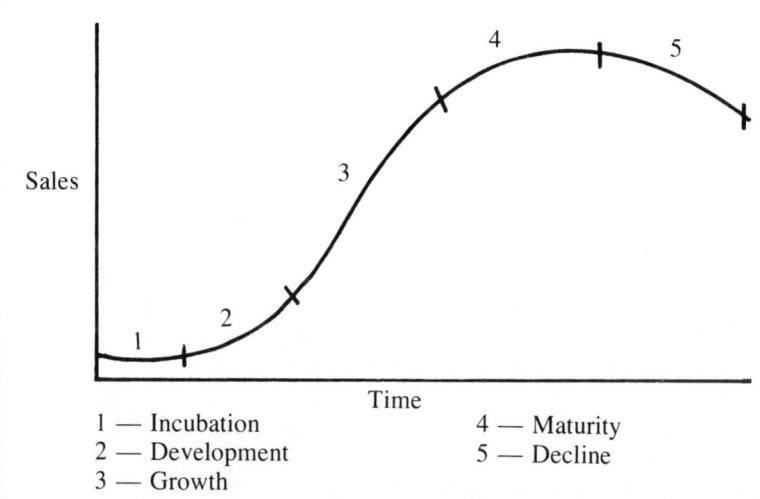

1 — Incubation   4 — Maturity
2 — Development   5 — Decline
3 — Growth

(1) The incubation phase encompasses the conceptual gestation of the product, including the basic idea and its perceived need or demand in the environment. It covers research and development, prototype and testing experiments, budgeting and initial commitment. In dealing with the unknown future, the early deliberations involve expectations more than facts. For this reason it is imperative that expectations be written down in order to test them against assumptions in the evolution of the product. Given the laws of probability for product failure, most new products will prove abortive and will never be presented in the test market.

(2) The development state marks its entry into a test market. Typically, the initial test sales will provide a feedback for possible retention or abandonment. Generally, the market development stage is characterized by little competition, high costs and thin profit margins. In short, the product will require a high degree of resources often without any substantial return. In this shakedown and shakeout period only a small minority of new product candidates will deserve the commitment for an all-out push.

(3) The growth phase signals the period of economic takeoff for the successful period. In shifting into high gear the product's revenue should greatly exceed its cost. At the same time when profits become noticeable in the marketplace, aggressive emulators appear on the scene contributing to market saturation.

(4) During the phase of maturity, revenue will still exceed cost but to a lesser degree. In this maturity stage, the basic economic vitality

tends to level off, the competition usually becomes more intense and demand falls off.

(5) In the stage of decline, the product requires greater promotional input, advertising, price rebates, and sales efforts, but there is usually a corresponding decrease in proportionate revenue characterized by a lower turnover and loss of consumer appeal.

According to Philip Kotler, Professor of Marketing at Northwestern University, in his examination of life cycle analysis, the stages of maturity and ultimate decline also provide an opportunity for prolonging the longevity of the product. He states that the object is to find: "(1) new uses for the product; (2) new product features and refinements; and (3) increased segmentation."[12]

Nylon fabric is a classic case for new ways to stimulate and regenerate sales at the maturity stage. Originally nylon was conceived for military use, particularly in providing rope and thread for parachutes. Subsequently, it replaced silk in the hosiery market. When that market declined, nylon, in 1945, was successfully introduced for warp knits in the textile industry, nylon cord tires in 1948, clothing textured yarns in 1955 and carpet yarns in 1959.

Other celebrated examples of product life extensions are Jello and Scotch Tape. In the case of Jello, General Foods extended the life span by emphasizing its benefit as a diet food. Initially the Minnesota Mining and Manufacturing Corporation conceived the use of Scotch Tape for book binding in libraries. Subsequently, it found the product had many other uses in the home. Finally, in centering its market research on housewives and children, thousands of new uses for Scotch Tape were discovered. On the other hand, management should speed the extinction of a product if convinced the product is becoming obsolete; then the product should not receive support in advertising, time, promotion, and good people.

The typewriter may be on the verge of obsolescence as a reproduction instrument. Today, it is much too slow for word processing uses. However, in terms of life cycle analysis it may still have great potential as a learning tool in the improvement of reading skills.

In the final stage of decline, one sign of the product's economic death is when the company has to spend ninety-eight cents of cost to achieve a dollar of revenue. Despite the contrived physical existence of this type of product through promotional activities, for all practical purposes, it is economically dead, and if it does not lend itself to rejuvenation the product should be promptly discontinued.

As in the case of other theoretical principles, it is much easier to recognize the value of the analytical tool than to practice the arduous task of application. Life cycle analysis is a very provocative idea, but in practice, it is difficult to apply because many managements are unaware where they are in the product's overall pattern. Understanding the pattern conceptually is fairly easy, but few managements have a sure grasp in categorizing the product into its fundamental stages of incubation, development, growth, maturity and decline.

Each stage in the product cycle requires a different set of strategies in prolonging the life span of the product. Unlike biological organisms, there is no strict law of duration, for the customer dictates the product's life or death. Applying the general framework of a product's life cycle makes it possible for the entrepreneur to allocate more rationally and to extend the life cycle by recognizing the interaction of the various phases. Although many marketing critics are correct in questioning a slavish adherence to life cycle theory, it has, nevertheless, the advantage of putting the product to the test of economic results and abandoning it at the most propitious time so that it will not absorb precious resources.

Segmentation

Segmentation analysis is another technique introduced into the entrepreneurial tool kit in recent years. Briefly, it runs counter to the conventional wisdom of perceiving a product or a service exclusively in terms of a homogeneous or broad mass market. Conversely, it identifies and divides customers into various categories, each with different characteristics and expectations. Although segmentation analysis does not ignore the contributions of market research in the areas of demographics, educational profiles, mobility, national income, or purchasing power, it views these aggregates as the foundation for a more probing analysis of a smaller market component.

The main premise of segmentation is its rejection of the notion that a universal homogeneous market exists. Successful companies in the beer, coffee, automotive and watch industries have successfully concentrated on segmentation to prove that consumer homogeneity is more myth than reality. The General Foods and General Motors corporations provide many types of coffee and automobiles to reach segmented markets. Segmentation also infers that there is no single way of developing a mass market; different company knowledge and perception argue that there are many different ways of approaching the market. Anheuser-

With affluence there is an accompanying shift from physical to psychological factors in the consumption patterns. This approach is really a marketing utilization of Abraham Maslow's psychological theory of various levels of human needs. He contends there is a gradation of hierarchy of overlapping needs ranging from "safety, belongingness, love, respect and self-esteem."[13] Applying Maslow's theory, the traditional distinction between a need and a want loses much of its former Busch Incorporated is clearly the leader in the beer industry, but there are other success stories. Coors, Pabst, the Jos. Schlitz Brewing Company and Miller are examples of firms applying segmentation analysis in looking at the market differently for economic results.

Engel's Law, developed by the nineteenth century German statistician Ernst Engel, is an additional aid in understanding market segmentation. It states that as family income increases, there will be a smaller percentage spent on food, fuel and household operations, but a higher percentage of disposable income on other items. In short, as the medium family income exceeds $14,000, disposable income on items beyond basic necessities will increase.

meaning. Normally a need is defined as something required to maintain sustenance, but this relates largely to the physical elements of survival and security which are basically more stable (assuming the absence of hyper-inflation) compared to the volatile psychic needs of success and satisfaction. In an affluent society where the necessities have been mastered, the psychological expectations become more important. Moreover, if one views a want as a perceived need, then Maslow's theory of hierarchical values becomes more individual and emotional.

In an affluent consumeristic society, this opens the door for many interpretations in the segmentation of products. In such a society diversity increasingly tends to replace homogeneity of taste. Three examples of broad economic change are already visible. First, the use of credit shapes a new type of consumer whose value system is more concerned with renting than ownership. One of the greatest, but least publicized, of Alfred P. Sloan's innovations, was the creation of the General Motors Acceptance Corporation in 1919. In an era when national credit was circumscribed and the banks were not interested in automobile financing, Sloan, a giant American businessman and mentor of the General Motors Corporation, shrewdly realized that credit was a major avenue in creating a customer for car purchases. In advancing his concept of class segmentation based on "a purchaser for every purse," he saw that credit was the instrument of fulfillment for a new type of customer interested in something more than pure transportation. Credit also accounts for the great rise in leasing and renting into today's economy.

Second, the affluent consumer buys according to expectations, considering income a restraint. This feature of buying according to expectations is especially relevant in the case of young adults who shape their purchasing patterns in terms of the income they expect to be earning five to ten years hence. Certain rug manufacturers, for example, were able to take advantage of the situation that young couples often had little extra money when they bought their first home. Consequently, they arranged for the carpet to be part of the mortgage payment, allowing small payments over a long period of time.

Third, the concept of discretionary time becomes more relevant suggesting that rather than a product the customer actually purchases a convenience (packaging or frozen foods) or an activity (boating, bowling and other forms of leisure). In the case of the former, time is the value added; in the case of the latter, the competition is another form of activity which competes against the consumer's disposable time. Whereas disposable income is theoretically unlimited, time—even for a millionaire—is a restraint. When time is factored into the marketing strategy a different form of utility for the product emerges.

Peter Drucker has recently suggested that today's economy may be undergoing a revolutionary change in market segmentation. Basing his conclusions on demographic dynamics, he visualizes three major market categories in the coming decade. First, the elderly, who are growing in percentage terms faster than any other group; second, the young adults, an offshoot of the World War II "baby boom," who are growing fastest in numbers; and, finally, the emergence of the two breadwinner family in which the working wife is now a feature in fifty percent of American homes. Moreover, she contributes around forty percent of family income, the portion usually budgeted for discretionary spending. Each of these three segments has distinct needs requiring different marketing approaches. According to Drucker, it is still too early to state with certainty that the satisfaction of the consumer needs of these three groups will rank with the post World War I emergence of class segmentation and the post World War II phenomenon of life style, but he contends it bears close scrutiny in the marketing plans of the nineteen eighties.[14]

Financial Planning

The opportunity for improving the productivity of capital rarely gets the attention it deserves from management; yet, it is a key to entrepreneurship. Although less visible than physical and human resources, the managing of capital is the easiest area to obtain results if management is sophisticated about what it is doing about making capital assets work more effectively. In the previous discussion of Pareto's law and transactional analysis, specific examples were cited for improving the productivity of capital by altering the product mix in order to sell a larger proportion of revenue producing items and through strategic warehousing in which the same amount of inventory supports a larger volume of sales.

In simple terms, the productivity of capital represents an input/output relationship among the cost/benefit ratios of all the factors of production, with the goal of obtaining the greatest output for the least effort. Productivity of capital is the area most companies give least attention, probably because management mistakenly believes that profitability adequately measures it.

In the recent past there has been a heavy emphasis on leverage manipulation and a host of other financial techniques, particularly by the conglomerates, to obtain greater mileage from capital resources. But, it is a fallacy to assume that buying profits is a sound policy for managing the assets of the business over the long run. Excessive emphasis on the bottom line is dangerous because it obscures the other survival functions of the business. The application of appropriate financial techniques (which is beyond the scope of this book) is important, but should only come into play after a sound financial strategy has been enunciated for the business.

After a period when it was considered unfashionable and embarrassing for a company to have cash reserves, management is shifting its emphasis toward liquidity. In order to take advantage of entrepreneurial opportunities, and obtain the fullest use of expensive capital, cash flow rather than earnings per share is becoming increasingly important. With the financial rationale shifting from maximization of profits and attractive price/earning ratios, the emphasis in the late nineteen seventies will be asset management on the minimization of the cost of capital. The stock market is mirroring this trend of financial performance. The star performers are those with the greatest cash flow.

Planning by Questions

Another example of starting with numbers instead of sound financial concepts is the false practice used in many companies introducing some percentage figure for return on investment, and then attempting to make the figures conform to that preconceived notion. The correct approach is to examine the most appropriate capital structure capable of providing minimum profitability and the minimum cost of capital. The

Entrepreneurial Tactics

approach of planning by questions involves the rejection of starting off with an aggregate figure and instead concentrating on the components making up the capital resource profile. The entrepreneurial pursuit of managing the capital resource more effectively means raising specific questions.

- How is investment defined?
- What are the main business areas in which capital is invested (machinery and equipment, inventory, receivables, supplier and finished goods, shelf space)?
- How much productive work does the capital invested in each sector contribute to overall results?
- How could these components be improved?
- What standards of measurement are applied in calculating the productivity of fixed and supporting capital?
- In what way does profitability (past and future costs) take into account bigger risks and opportunities?
- To what extent is profitability creating tomorrow's jobs?
- How much working capital is needed to survive a short term financial panic of three to four months?
- What is the time period established for optimum earnings?
- Does the financial strategy factor in inflation when measuring economic results?
- What are the financial controls for measuring the economic results, such sub-aggregates as: receivables, credit, physical resources, human resources, etc.?
- How is management considering the relationship of turnover of money and profit margin?
- Does management know within reasonable range what its future cost requirements will be in terms of manpower, distribution, plant expansion, inventory, research, and labor negotiations?
- Is management exploring the various alternatives for measuring profitability (return on assets, return on investments, profit on sales) and what is the best yardstick?
- What are the costs of non-productivity, i.e., equipment and space not being adequately used within the business?
- What is the responsibility of operating people in managing the performance of money?[15]

Karl Marx's prediction on the eventual demise of capitalism rested on his inexorable law of the diminishing return on capital. The successful entrepreneurial accomplishments by business in the past have contributed in large measure to blunting Marx's forecast. In pursuing the risk taking entrepreneurial function of coupling the application of capital with technological and social innovations, management has been able to introduce new products, elevate the standard of living and expand the work force. When Marx died in 1883, he had no idea that entrepreneurs would be creating up to World War I major new industries at the rate of approximately one every three years. Nevertheless, the logic of his prophetic arguments on the productivity of capital continue to have a haunting reality for the system. Modern management can move thoroughly to puncture Marx's prediction by directing capital into areas of opportunity and by responding more effectively to the challenges of the aforementioned financial questions. One thing is certain in the business environment of the late nineteen seventies: the productivity of capital cannot be taken for granted. In addition to demanding as much attention as the management of human and physical resources, it will also require that financial analysts display an entrepreneurial point of view.

The People Area

Entrepreneurship is not exclusively a superfunction dependent on top management fiat. Permeating the entire business, it demands action, implementation and performance by marketing, accounting, production and personnel groups within the organization. Unless people recognize the vision and understand the objectives of the business, serious imbalances will result in coordination, communication and control. Without a firm expression of confidence from top management, a confident and courageous outlook by executives toward tomorrow and proper staffing, the chances of taking advantage of the most attractive opportunity will be an exercise in rhetoric. This requires each manager supplementing his role as an administrator; it entails thinking and acting as an entrepreneur. If a positive corporate atmosphere is created for encouraging change and rewarding participants for results, entrepreneurship has the tendency to breed further entrepreneurship. The experience of Minnesota Mining and Manufacturing Company and other corporate innovators confirms this point.

Because the human dimension of entrepreneurship will be treated in fuller depth in the following chapter, I shall not go beyond identifying its importance and making a few general observations.

One approach in engendering the entrepreneurial spirit is to make every division a profit center in the performance of the whole business. A key guideline in the process is that new products should get the best there is in the way of company talent. Also, in staffing from strength, it often makes more sense to assign responsibility to younger talent who can bring fresh energy and perception to the task. A common mistake is combining strong and able men with their average and mediocre counterparts; this is a form of entrepreneurial dilution that rarely works. Neither does the practice of giving the competent man more and more to do. Eventually, it will result in the ineffectiveness of the able man and the failure of the project.

External Resources

As a business grows in size, diversity and complexity, an accompanying addition in new knowledge needs is inevitable. Business growth also dictates a proportionate increase of environmental encounters requiring new areas of corporate specialization. In confronting these new challenges there will always be the temptation for reasons of internal control and corporate ego to respond to these new knowledge requirements by adding to the internal staff. However, given the scarcity of competent human resources, it is improbable that a business has sufficient talent to service properly all the internal and environmental demands.

From an entrepreneurial standpoint it is probably wiser to farm out things that fall outside its knowledge competency and that it absolutely does not have to do. In the long run it reduces cost and is probably more effective for total performance. For those things that require a detached outside view (public relations, advertising, accounting audit, market research, legal services, executive education, etc.) the use of external resources takes on an added validity. Normally, those things requiring an outside viewpoint cannot be done effectively from the inside because once installed within the organizational framework there is the tendency for the individual or group working on the function to become part of the establishment, making it almost mandatory to adopt the perceptions and perspectives of top management. A substantive benefit derived from using outsiders is that it avoids the vulnerability of organizational incest by presenting corporate alternatives in the decision making process. Attempting to do everything inside the business creates the additional danger of erecting superfluous staffs, which, in the tradition of Parkinson's law, grow into paralyzing bureaucracies. Finally, size alone confers no economic distinction. Economic results emerge from being effective and bureaucracy is usually a deterrent in achieving this objective.[16]

The utilization of external resources has particular relevance in make-buy decisions. In the expanding complexity of modern big business, the important thing is reasonable control of the general process from raw materials to customer. This does not necessarily include ownership of all stages in the process. Doing everything within the process adds to risk and effort and detracts from opportunities. This is particularly true when what is being done through integration does not fit the knowledge excellences of the business. Through its powerful purchasing policy Sears Roebuck and Company exerts indirect control of product design over thousands of suppliers, indicating it would be foolish to opt for ownership. Its knowledge resides in expert purchasing procedures and knowing what the consumer wants, which it demands of all its suppliers. Sears Roebuck resisted the temptation of needless empire building, but utilized instead its ability to be paid over and over again for its knowledge excellences of design and purchasing.

On the other hand, if a company vitally needs a specific dimension of knowledge, then the best path is the merger rather than in trying to pull itself up by its own knowledge bootstraps. In short, the secret of a successful merger policy is the use of available money to buy precious time and hard earned experience. It means purchasing what somebody else has taken years to develop in order to avoid the frustrations of blending a new knowledge dimension to the existing business. The bricks, mortar and machinery are least important compared to the time, talent and experience dimensions in conducting a make-buy decision.

CHAPTER V

Approaches to Managerial Effectiveness

INTRODUCTION

OCEANS of ink have been poured on the important subject of improving executive performance; most of it, ironically, by individuals who have had little or no direct exposure to the rigors of the administrative or entrepreneurial process. In the complex and confusing realm of executive effectiveness three major viewpoints prevail: organizational and behavioral theory; the guerrilla fighters; and the cynics.

Organizational and Behavioral Theory

Research in the area of organizational and behavioral theory is by far the most comprehensive and searching. The theories include the endorsement of formal organizational principles (authority equals responsibility, line and staff, the span of control and the hierarchical organizational chart) drawn chiefly from military and ecclesiastical models. Supplementing traditional organizational theory are the proposed implementing factors of planning, organizing, coordinating and controlling which originated from early management theory.

During the past two generations, executives have been subject to a host of human relation panaceas which became fashionable for a time, but which, after losing their initial luster, melted into the forgotten limbo of most fads. Among the most notable in the long list are: the role of the informal organization, managerial grids, the phenomenon of sensitivity training, T-groups and encounter sessions, transactional analysis, participatory management, general system theory, the role of hierarchical managerial needs, Theory X and Theory Y, modern communication theory, creativity seminars and decision making simulation. At some time during their careers, captive executive audiences have been exposed, in various management development programs, to many of these concepts.

Encompassed within this vast panorama of print, many probing scholars have produced provocative ideas and have illuminated their concepts with rich clinical evidence. At the same time the confused executive practitioner, faced with the daily challenges of action, must objectively conclude that never had we owed so little to so many in terms of actual results. Measured in terms of research output, if any positive correlation existed between the plethora of theories and their translation into meaningful results, then the problem of executive effectiveness would quickly vanish. Despite the intellectual stimulation of many of the theories, they often lose their glow in the sharp light of operating reality.

What accounts for the wide gap between theory and reality? Two interrelated factors suggest the inadequacy of the theorists. First, there is the passionate belief on the part of many of the behaviorists that they have monistic answers. In raising false expectations they oversimplify complexity with the result that many of their potentially useful concepts are buried in the management journals under the raging debates between schools of thought. In any given month, the curious manager will find rich supporting evidence for a particular theory; and in the following month, he will be treated to counter documentation assailing the previous theory. It is small wonder that as the debates rage the puzzled executive believes he is a victim of the "publish or perish" syndrome of academe.

Second, there is the element of organization myopia in that the business enterprise is viewed by the behaviorists exclusively as a human organization. In this one dimensional tunnel vision of human organization, the other survival functions of marketing, finance, research and the environment are conveniently ignored by the behavioral scientists. Consequently, much of the relevance is lost. In the works of Douglas McGregor, Chris Argyris, Frederick Herzberg, Abraham Maslow, to cite only a few, the committed professional can mine many nuggets of understanding in promoting his effectiveness in general and obtain a better understanding of himself in particular. Unfortunately, in doing so, he must cut through the semantics of academic debate and disassociate himself from the monistic mythology confronting him. Many of the concepts are important for self-knowledge but there are no panaceas. Each manager must privately reconcile theory and practice in terms of his individual motivation. Because motivation is a major focus of psychological theory, it will be treated in greater depth as a separate section of this chapter.

The Guerrilla Fighters

The second category dealing with managerial effectiveness is advanced by a group of literary "agent provocateurs" who hope to blast away the smug hypocrisy of current theory and practice. In its satirical and witty forays, this group wages a type of guerrilla warfare by making the large organizational establishments the butt of its jokes. As a mirror of the school's popularity, several of its votaries (C. Northcote Parkinson, Laurence Peter, Anthony Jay and Robert Townsend)[1] have scaled the heights of the best seller lists.

Cleverly attacking the insouciance of bureaucracy, irreverently hurling barbs at the pretentiousness of managers, adroitly exposing the arrogance of academics, and brilliantly depicting with caustic humorous examples the pompousness of various executive types, these writers provide us with entertaining reading and a pleasant escape from daily pressures. If nothing else, in terms of entrepreneurial thinking, they remind us of the dangers of taking ourselves too seriously in the midst of ignorance, uncertainty and complexity. But when the laughs fade away and reality re-emerges, they leave us without a feasible alternative in the quest for executive effectiveness. Being told what is wrong and what is ridiculous about the organizational milieu has its therapeutic side effects, but it is no substitute for providing us meaningful guidelines in seeking new opportunities and improving executive performance.

The Cynics

The cynics represent the final school of thought on executive effectiveness. Since they reflect a distinct mood, they have, fortunately or unfortunately, left no great literature in their wake. In making a virtue of their intellectual ignorance, they remain totally unconvinced of the worth of any theory related to practice. According to J. Samuel Bois, the semantics scholar: "They see theorists as experts who are given freedom to speculate in their think tanks or their laboratories, but whose intervention in the affairs of men should be accepted or refused, controlled and managed by men of practical experience, whose sober judgment is not contaminated by any 'isms.' "[2] Imbued with a narcissistic image of "the self-made man," the cynics contend that all great administrators and entrepreneurs are baptized in infancy with a charismatic blessing of leadership grace, concluding that after God made them as models, He threw away the mold.

With their contempt for all theory, the cynics are blinded by the fallacy of the indispensable man. Responding to the ancient question of whether managers are born or made, they readily acknowledge that the first half of the statement is palpably true. Moreover, they are totally confirmed in the belief that with their unique indigenous value system and special configuration of genes and chromosomes, nature has already blessed them with all the traits and ingredients of entrepreneurial leadership. The Carlylean prototype of the hero may have had some relevance when organizations were small and essentially the extension of one man, but in a world of rapid change and complexity, it becomes reduced to a myth. In the large organization of today no man is indispensable; instead we have a reality in which everybody is needed but nobody is needed too much.

Experience is important but managerial productivity and performance go beyond any single clinical dimension. As Sebastian Chamfort, the eighteenth century French dramatist, pointed out: "Man arrives at every stage of life as a novice." The purpose of the organization is to make people with different knowledges effective so that the individual parts become greater than the whole. In the concept of organizational perpetuity, the institution transcends the life span of any single individual. To survive, an organization needs theoretical concepts and guidelines, and it makes no sense to throw the theoretical baby out of the institutional bath. The concept of viewing the enterprise as a shadowy extension of one man is a fallacy. Moreover, in fostering the cult of omniscience, it perpetuates the notion of one man top management and removes the ingredient of trust and cooperation so crucial for performing entrepreneurial tasks.

MOTIVATION

Motivation has received major attention in the academic and business world as the principal key to managerial effectiveness.

Definition

Motivation has been the glamor word among psychologists and businessmen, which was expected hopefully to unlock the mysteries of work productivity and personal achievement. In the pursuit of the holy grail of fulfillment, psychologists have been splitting semantical hairs on the meaning of motivation with the vigor of medieval scholastic theologians proving the existence of God.

Despite the intellectual assault on the search for the meaning of motivation, the concept stubbornly resists a satisfactory definition. A consensus among scholars defines motivation as a process whereby managers attempt to stimulate through job satisfaction the fulfillment of human needs in order to simultaneously meet the goals of the organization and the individual. Notice the use of such evocative words as process, stimulate, satisfaction, needs, fulfillment, along with personal and institutional goals, all signifying emotionally charged interpretations depending on the viewpoint of the user. Although the definition appears generally sound, in trying to translate it into performance, it obscures as much as it illuminates. At the same time, it is impossible to escape the conclusion that without motivation, work becomes meaningless. Managers have no alternative but to accept the reality of imprecise definition, while pursuing a deeper understanding of motivation.

Interpretations

Two major streams of thought, each with countless rivulets, dominate the literature of motivation. In general, most psychologists have navigated the stormy waters by opting for either the external or internal route of interpretation. The former, concentrating on the without, explores external stimuli as the main avenue shaping human behavior. The oldest approach in this category, focusing on the within, in charting the motives of inner man, attempts to channel such subjective factors as personal satisfaction, need, fulfillment and expectation; and thereby, steer the individual in the direction of greater fulfillment.

The external approach owed much to the pioneering experiments of John Watson and Ivan Pavlov who produced the first systematic attempt to weave a motivational theory around the threads of stimulus and response. B. F. Skinner,[3] the Harvard psychologist, is currently the leading advocate of this school of thought. The rudimentary theory of stimulus and response is characterized by basic simplicity. Soft pedaling the feature of passion and purpose in human activities, it assumes desired behavior is possible through a pattern of human engineering which derives its source of reinforcement from external stimuli. According to the theorists of this persuasion, the implementation of desired behavior occurs in two basic ways: altering the environmental factors bearing on the conditions of work, or through manipulative human engineering (communication, training, persuasion, etc.). The classic illustration of stimulus and response theory is the carrot and stick analogy, which conditions a person to do something by promising rewards, but failing in that approach the coercive feature of punishment enters the act.

The research findings produced by psychologists in this field are not entirely invalid. Significant contributions, particularly in the realm of physiological motives, have resulted from their clinical experiments. Among the most notable contributions are in the areas dealing with fatigue, boredom, food deprivation, alcoholic and narcotic intake, the categorization of harmful stimuli and the need for a favorable climate in promoting stimulating activities. At the same time behavioral psychologists have been severely criticized for their physiological parochialism in laboring the obvious, placing undue stress on the observable and ignoring the drives of inner man. By concentrating on the measurable and quantitative, they have neglected the qualitative dimension of man and have failed to provide much illumination on the deeper nature of work, particularly knowledge work. Given the basic assumption of this school of thought, it is difficult to imagine major contributions meeting the needs of post industrial society. Moreover, if we accept Skinner's thesis of the myth of autonomous man, the price of this type of human engineering may be too big for a democratic society to pay.

The great trail blazer of the internal school of thought was Sigmund Freud, who was primarily concerned with what was taking place inside the mind of individuals, particularly with their unconscious drives. Freud's comprehensive theory, which underwent frequent revision, can only be sketched in broad strokes. From a psychoanalytical point of view, he saw motivation and its accompanying behavior as a product of conflicting individual drives, needs and expectations, along with the abilities of people to cope with them in terms of reality. According to Freud, an individual's personality traits emerge from inner tensions within the structure of the psyche and the demands for socialization. His concepts were so revolutionary that he was forced to introduce a new vocabulary of the mind. Accordingly, he separated the personality into three belligerent segments: the *id*, the *ego*, and the *superego*.

Arguing that behavior is essentially determined from repressed sexuality, Freud saw the *id* as the unconscious seat of instinctual drives in the selfish pursuit of the pleasure principle. For example, the initial responses of the infant are motivated by his selfish needs for body satisfactions. However, as he becomes less and less dependent with maturity, he is forced to come to terms with a new stage of reality. The second element or *ego*, playing the role of a referee or mental mediator, operates on a secondary but more conscious level; it adjusts to reality in terms of enlightened self-interest. It is the ego's task to moderate and control the primitive passions and pressures of the *id*. The *ego* attempts to cope with and survive in the outside world by suppressing the anarchic impulses of the *id*. Moreover, the ego ideal represents a source of personal identity or an internalized image of one's self at its putative best in terms of personality fulfillment and actualization.

The final segment of Freud's personality trinity is the *superego*, a spiritual gyroscope serving as the individual's conscience. According to Harry Levinson, President of the Levinson Institute, the *superego* conducts four interrelated functions: the acquisition of rules, the evolution of values, the aspiration of the ego idea and self-judgment. The *superego* infringes on the *ego* by arousing guilt feelings when the latter seeks to express *id* impulses. Consequently, in coping with reality, the *ego* must respond to the demands of the *superego* or conscience as well as the selfish instincts of the *id*. For Freud, anxiety is the inevitable outcome among the three working elements in the personality structure. At the same time, this inevitable conflict provides the basis of motivation. Since the *id* cannot always achieve its objectives, motivational energy develops in the form of sublimation and displacement as a result of the rivalry between the pleasure and reality principles, the tension between dependence and independence, and the search for identity. Finally, since no two persons have the same personality dynamics, each person has different ministration (dependence on the outside) and maturity needs (the factors of growth and fulfillment).[4]

Freud is essentially pessimistic regarding human improvement through motivation. Although neuroses can be alleviated by psychoanalysis, a person will change his behavior only when he has something to gain through self-justification. Intellectual debates continue to rage around his ideas on motivation, but one thing is certain—they serve as a counterweight to the empirical tradition of the behaviorists.

Recent Thinkers

In recent years psychologists were supposed to come to the rescue of businessmen by refining and applying the concepts of motivation in order to increase productivity and make workers achieve more. To what extent they succeeded is still a subject of debate, but their efforts are worth exploring.

Abraham Maslow

In his two major works, *Toward a Psychology of Being* and *Motivation and Personality*, Maslow, as a neo-Freudian, sees internal motives as the major factor affecting change and human behavior. Acknowledging his debt to Freud, he claims, however, that the father of psychoanalysis was unduly concerned with the pathological and neurotic features of man. Maslow sets out to redress this imbalance by concentrating on the healthy side of man's personality. His motivational theory centers on need gratification which he considers the key to motivation and human development.[5]

Maslow envisages the human being growing and maturing, and hence, motivating himself, by passing through various stages of need fulfillment. He visualizes needs as forming a hierarchical pattern in which after the fulfillment of a person's lower needs, then higher needs assume increased importance. In examining the need for physical safety and proceeding to economic security, love, social esteem and self-actualization, Maslow conceptualizes human needs in the following dynamic fashion: "We have seen that the chief principle of organization in human organizational life is the arrangement of his basic needs in a hierarchy of less or greater priority of potency. The chief dynamic principle motivating the organization is the emergence in the healthy person of less potent needs upon the gratification of more potent ones."[6]

Based on his hierarchy of need gratification, Maslow suggests three general conclusions: First, the impossibility of motivating anyone by appealing to a need that has been adequately satisfied. Second, rejecting manipulation and homogeneity of needs, motivational understanding requires flexibility, depending on the situation, because each individual will have different needs at different times. Third, although the pattern of motivation is general, motivation is always specific, and it is the job of the manager to determine the particular need.

Maslow, for example, assigned economic wants toward the base of the pyramid, suggesting that once an economic want is satisfied the less future monetary satisfaction matters. But apparently what Maslow failed to recognize fully in the application of his pyramidical premises is that a need itself changes in the act of being satisfied and contains dynamic rather than static imperatives of its own. To conclude, for example, that when economic needs are satisfied, the quest for further economic gain becomes irrelevant, is misleading. Economic rewards continue to play an important role in need gratification, but for non-economic reasons. Moreover, if economic benefits are not forthcoming there is a tendency to create dissatisfaction leading to the destruction of motivation. Specifically, the differing salaries of executive vice presidents, while adequate in meeting economic needs, continue to have significance, in which case pay becomes part of the status and esteem dimension rather than one of economic manifestation. What takes place is a form of marginal utility. The additional economic increment needed to satisfy must not only be more but a good deal more.

Saul Gellerman in his book, *Management by Motivation*, notes the relationship between economic reward and status needs when he points out that a monetary need can never be described in a totally objective way, despite the fact that it may be quantitatively cited in dollar terms. All increments are relative depending on a variety of factors: existing income, expectations, past pattern of income growth and personal estimation of worth. In general, the more he is accustomed to receiving increments, the larger the income required to impress him. Gellerman concludes that money is not omnipotent but neither is it impotent. In a world of ingrates it perhaps acts more as a dissatisfier if it is not forthcoming. Given the reality of expectations most people will spend their careers in a comparative state of dissatisfaction with pay.[7] In this sense the alleged economic need which Maslow places low in his scale is never really fulfilled.

Maslow is a provocative thinker to whom we owe a debt of gratitude for his searching insights, but he falls prey to oversimplification. Perhaps he is irrefutable, if one accepts his static principle of hierarchical needs as totally valid. However, this is impossible since individual motivation is a complex pattern of stimuli and cognition, personality, and perception which fail to blend into the five neat categories outlined by Maslow. Moreover, he never comes to grips with a fully satisfactory explanation of self-actualization, the apex of his pyramid.

Frederick Herzberg

Arguing that meaningful gratification depends on satisfying in differing degrees, external and internal needs, Herzberg divides the concept of motivation into two main categories—the intrinsic and the extrinsic. Although he sees the role for both types of needs, he considers the intrinsic qualitatively more important than the extrinsic.

Accordingly, in the intrinsic realm, he lists the major contributions to motivation as: achievement, responsibility, recognition (along with opportunity for advancement and promotion), autonomy and independence, participation in problem solving and the work itself.

Among the principal extrinsic factors affecting motivation, he cites the following: money, working conditions, fringe benefits, position and rank, job security, and supervision.[8]

Herzberg labels the extrinsic factors as hygienic and less important to motivation because of their ephemeral nature and because they reside outside the individual's control in being rendered by somebody else. Since hygienic factors, according to Herzberg, are only peripherally related to the job and the task, they are not potent in providing strong motivational meaning to the individual. In essence, Herzberg maintains that the hygienic factors play a pivotal role in dissatisfying and discomforting the individual when they are absent. He contends that people are never permanently satisfied with a raise. And in due course, merit raises are expected as a matter of seniority right rather than performance. Even less satisfying for genuine motivation are the privilege and status features of the job.[9]

Herzberg maintains there is nothing wrong in providing maximum hygiene features for employees, but he argues that management has been shortsighted in thinking it could fulfill human needs by the exclusive improvement of these extrinsic factors. Considering them addictive and of short duration, he states, "Hygiene acts like heroin—it takes more and more to produce less and less effect."[10] Consequently, the neglect of the intrinsic features and the promotion of hygienic features can be, in the long run, only counterproductive and lead to false expectations. In pointing out the limitations of hygienic needs, he remarks:

> It is clear the hygiene needs fail to provide for positive satisfactions; they do not possess the characteristics necessary for giving an individual a sense of growth. To feel that one has grown depends on achievement in tasks that have meaning to the individual and since the hygiene factors do not relate to the task they are powerless to give such meaning to the individual. Growth is dependent on some achievements, but achievement requires a task. The motivators are task factors and thus are necessary for growth; they provide the psychological stimulation by which the individual can be activated toward his self-realization needs.[11]

As a general theorist, Herzberg has perhaps the most relevance for businessmen. He is aware of the limitations and complexity of motivating others, recognizes the importance of intrinsic and extrinsic factors, and has done outstanding research work in attempting to understand the motives of knowledge professionals. Perhaps the major contribution of Herzberg is his recognition of the role of work and achievement in fostering motivation. The importance of this factor will be amplified in the next chapter.

Douglas McGregor
One of the most celebrated books in business literature is *The*

Approaches to Managerial Effectiveness

Human Side of Enterprise by Douglas McGregor, in which he sees the hinge of motivation swinging around the theme of managerial styles. The main thrust of the work rests on his two interpretations about the worker's human nature which he designates as "theory X" and "theory Y." According to the assumptions of "theory X," management views people in the work force as inherently lazy, shunning responsibility, disliking work and fearing commitment. On the other hand, "theory Y" assumes an antithetical interpretation of human nature, stressing that the worker is self-starting, welcomes responsibility and endorses the work ethic.[12]

Since McGregor only describes and provides no empirical evidence, it is difficult to determine if he has proven anything. He offers no proof that a "theory Y" organization will actually outperform a "theory X" one, except that the former is undoubtedly a much more congenial place to work.

In depicting the motivational technique associated with the paternalistic managerial style of "theory X," he exposes many of its motivational vulnerabilities. For example, the main approaches for anyone pursuing the assumptions of "theory X" are:

1. Power—better do it my way because I say so.
2. Authoritative manipulation—since I am the boss I know best. Because the boss does not make mistakes, therefore, it is just and proper to coerce the worker into performance.
3. A vulgarized version of the carrot and the stick by pressing the buttons of rewards and punishment for results. If the worker does as the superior suggests it will please him; if not, he can expect punishment, chastisement and rebuke.
4. Money—an appeal to greed suggesting it is possible to obtain results by creating an army of mercenaries within the firm.
5. Paternalism—assumption that everybody is part of one big happy family sharing company goals; and therefore, making it redundant to emphasize motivation.

McGregor contends that these ancient motivational techniques go back to the pyramid builders, but he also suggests they still exist in covert forms and more refined versions in the minds of many managements. McGregor's sympathies clearly lie with the assumption of the "theory Y" model, which endorses responsibility, encourages decision making and fosters participative democracy within the organization. Probably because McGregor's ideas meshed neatly with the political values of American democracy, his book received a great deal of endorsement among both academics and businessmen during the decades of the fifties and sixties. Since business has been continually criticized for being anti-democratic, McGregor's ideas proved irresistable. If participative democracy could also produce economic results, then this would really be the tribute that vice paid to virtue.

It is doubtful, however, if McGregor and his votaries recognized the full implications of "theory Y" assumptions. Upon deeper consideration, the appealing assumptions should not be taken at their face value. First, talent is anti-democratic and anti-egalitarian. It is inhumane for the weak who are constitutionally unable to cope with the rigors and discipline connected with it. Moreover, McGregor incorrectly assumes that the world is populated by mature adults. Second, contrary to the premises of "theory Y," the strong and the healthy also need the assurances of organizational security. Participative democracy can easily disintegrate into participative chaos. Legitimate authority is needed, particularly in crisis situations as a cement for the bonds of work. Third, contrary to its postulates, "theory Y" will never really be as permissive as it claims to be in practice. Responsibility and freedom, like Siamese twins, are impossible to separate. Rather than being free from restraint, individual responsibility is a demanding taskmaster.

Finally, all theories about human nature are deceptive. In suggesting that human nature is divisible into two neat packages, McGregor exposes his theory to a special vulnerability. Although it is true that there are lazy and dedicated people in any organization, it is even more important to note that people will not act the same at all times. The situation and the roles will often determine the action; people will respond quite differently under various conditions. In certain circumstances they may sabotage (either consciously or unconsciously); in other situations they may achieve brilliant feats of performance. All of which suggests there are many human natures which foster different behavior depending on the challenge, the task and the job. Raising the issue of a dual human nature is misleading; the real question is the reality of the work situation.

Chris Argyris

From Chris Argyris' interpretation of motivational reality one central premise stands out; namely, that the needs of the present day business organization and the wants of the individual follow incongruous paths.[13] Argyris poses the dichotomy in the following way:

> As I suggested at the beginning, the typical formal organization, administrative controls, and directive leadership may

tend to inveigh against individual mental health and induce individuals to aspire toward dependency, submissiveness, etc., or create informal activities that lead them to become apathetic, indifferent, and eventually alienated. . . .[14]

Although he maintains it is not possible to create an organization wherein the individual needs and organizational demands are in complete agreement, he does feel it is possible to create the "axiologically good" organization which is conducive to improving individual capacity and mental health. Argyris has made important empirical contributions and many of his suggestions have considerable merit, but his idealistic aspirations of having organizations without alienation indicates that his aspirations exceed his knowledge. Although he is not directly responsible, he has opened the door to many new fads and techniques attempting to fill the knowledge gaps between the ideal of mental health and superior performance with organizational realities. Sensitivity training, which consists of small encounter group interaction under conditions of stress requiring the participants to become attuned to each other's feelings, is one of the most novel psychotherapeutic techniques to improve motivation emanating from this hypothesis.

In their quest for the "axiologically good" organization, Argyris and other psychologists are paradoxically adopting "theory X" techniques from "theory Y" premises. In focusing on the search for awareness and the identity connected with the "real me," in the hope of avoiding alienation imposed by organizational demands, there is an implicit tendency to build into the system a revulsion and rejection for orderly and rational authority within the organization. Psychotherapists depict role as more important than goals. William Glasser complains: "The institutions of our society still operate as if goal took precedence over role."[15]

The organization and individual have two different logics, each mirroring specific tension and conflict. It is the job of management to harmonize these turbulences. Despite the best of intentions, the quixotic hope for the "axiological good organization" can only lead to a divorce.

A more serious criticism of this approach is that it will inevitably produce undesired outcomes. The desire for the "axiological good organization" operates under the romantic guise that the individual is controlling his own destiny. Since it is axiomatic that organizational power never operates in a vacuum, the real control quickly (whether intentionally or not) falls into the hands of others. It is hardly surprising that those psychologists who object most vehemently to coercive control by others end up by manipulating others.

Jean Jacques Rousseau, the arch philosophical proponent of "doing your own thing," was under no illusion about the power relationships. In his celebrated pedagogical treatise, *Emile*, Rousseau gave the following advice to teachers:

> Let the child believe he is in control, though it is always you [the teacher] who really controls. There is no subjugation as that which keeps the appearance of freedom. The poor baby knows nothing, able to do nothing. . . .[16]

Many modern psychologists with the best of intentions place unlimited faith in the benevolence of others, but benevolence is no guarantee against the abuse of power.

Substituting the democratic assumptions of "theory Y" for the harsher techniques of "theory X" is no panacea. Its inevitable result is psychological despotism. Psychologists preach sermons about the whole man, job enrichment, personal growth, absence of alienation, mental health and other high ideals, but under the umbrella of this rhetoric they practice insidious manipulation. Despite all their complaints about the juvenile treatment accorded employees in traditional organizations, they practice a similar paternalism using different techniques. Assuming that man is sick and filled with all types of frustration and neuroses, they conclude he does not want to achieve and wants to fail. Consequently, he desires to be controlled as a result of psychological alienation. But instead of using the old carrot and stick to reduce fear and hunger, the psychologists promise the incentive of psychological salvation by applying the sacraments of psychological techniques.

William T. Powers warns of the dangers facing the manipulator both to himself and others, when he concludes: ". . . attempts to control behavior—one's own or that of other people—accomplishes nothing in the long run, but produces conflict and consequent pathology."[17] Peter Drucker argues that if the Federal Drug Administration rules for safety were applied to psychotherapy all the panaceas would vanish. Regarding sensitivity training, he states:

> I'm one of those very simple people who believe that one is not entitled to inflict damage on the human body. For the weak, the lame, the defenseless, the shy, the vulnerable, this is a very dangerous thing. The real sadists, the wolves, tear the little lambs to pieces. The casualty rate is unacceptable.[18]

Psychological despotism suffers from the same defects as political despotism. It adopts the fallacy that omniscient philosopher kings exist. It naively argues that the search for absolute fulfillment, freedom and happiness are viable. It intrudes on the personal privacy of the individual. It argues that managers, acting as amateur psychologists, are healthy, knowledgeable and correct, whereas everybody else is different, indifferent, ignorant and stupid.[19]

This criticism has perhaps been unduly severe. There is no doubt that the psychologists are sincere, and maybe this is part of the trouble. It would be better, like Rousseau, if they were more aware of power dimensions of what they are doing. Unfortunately the wrong focus contained in many of the new teachings represents a gross abuse of psychology. From benevolent premises emerge despotic practices. The psychologists correctly assume that men want to work and contribute, at least in certain circumstances; but in translating this goal into action, they assume it will take place only if authority is diluted. Executive and professional work is demanding, so much so that more is needed than a genuflection to desire and the assertion of banal sincerity. In the long run such an approach, as Professor Adam Ulam of Harvard University, has pointed out in speaking of the new practice of university governance, will undermine authority, alienate everybody, and destroy the mission of the organization.[20] The fundamental purpose of psychology remains the same: to know how people behave and how we behave individually—but such an objective is impossible when motivation is addressed through psychological despotism.

Conclusion

The preceding survey of motivational theory shows that psychologists have failed to come to the rescue by providing management with sound principles in meeting the problem of making the worker achieve more and improve productivity. Nevertheless, there are many useful insights in the literature from which the manager may draw general conclusions.

It is the better part of wisdom to admit forthrightly that the issue of human nature and the complexity of human motives contains a good deal of mystery. Few have captured the difficulty of understanding the challenge better than Blaise Pascal, when he wrote:

> What a chimera is man! What confused chaos! What a subject of contradictions! A professed judge of all things, and

yet a feeble worm on earth! The great depositary and guardian of truth and yet a bundle of uncertainties! The glory and the shame of the universe![21]

Motivational theories of behavior are characterized by the feature of explaining behavior rather than teaching and applying it for corporate results. Except in the hands of expertly trained psychologists, the theories are highly speculative and provide little in the way of guidelines for action.

Although motivational theory is inadequate in assisting us to manage others, it contains many rich and instructive insights into one's own personality and it helps confirm the assumption that the only person one can manage is oneself.

Motivational theory is useful in assisting us to think through not so much what motivates people, but what destroys motivation. Perhaps, as a result, we know more about what ruins motivation than what creates it. Specifically, some of the things that dampen the ardor of motivation are:

1. Uncertainty about one's place in the organization and what is expected.
2. Unclear corporate and individual objectives.
3. Viewing people from preconceived monistic images (economic man, "theory X" and "theory Y, etc.) which often result in self-fulfilling prophecies.
4. Dealing with the work force as aggregates, without recognizing the factor of individual differences.
5. The recognition that most motives are learned from anticipation of goal-directed states; few motives are innate or natural.
6. Motives are pluralistic in both numbers and nature and they change with achievement and performance.
7. Conscious and unconscious motives tend to interact; men are neither perfectly rational nor perfectly instinctual, but imperfectly both.

At the present stage of our knowledge it is prudent to assume that managers cannot teach or program for motivation. Because managers must be accountable and perform in the present, they do not have the luxury of time to wait until psychologists provide them with answers. The best that managers can do is use the motivational knowledge they have by preparing for it and recognizing it when it takes place. They can prepare for it by their own self-development and note its presence when individuals or groups demonstrate achievement.

Approaches to Managerial Effectiveness

Motivation is important in providing behavior with energy and allowing a person to do what he thought he was previously incapable of doing. Hygienic factors and rewards also have their place. However, assuming the existence of basic economic and survival needs, the task or the job is the determining factor which should precede inner motives and extrinsic factors. Managers should concentrate on applying the little they know about motivation around job behavior and job results.[22] The job may not be everything but in an institution focusing on economic results, it realistically should come first. Poor hygienic factors can destroy achievement but if the job itself is ill-defined for performance, even the most ideal working conditions are fruitless. Job performance, not making people happy or trying to make them so through amateur psychology, is a prime task of entrepreneurial management. If one wants to change behavior, one does a better job by defining what result is sought in seeking corporate opportunities in order to meet the needs and demands of society. Of course, in pursuing economic tasks, the executive must avoid becoming "a workaholic," i.e., by becoming so involved in work that it interferes with his private life and destroys his humanity. This is too big a price to pay for success. In identifying what he wants to change in terms of accountability, the manager will soon recognize that behavior creates the role and not vice versa.

People change their behavior everyday by successfully accomplishing job tasks, but this is not the same as trying to alter personality. After a certain age only God can change personality and it is best to leave it to His wisdom. Economic performance is the true area of managerial competence and where the insights of psychology help in this task they are all to the good. A modest approach is far sounder than relying on panaceas and building false expectations.

Although it is fruitless to expect final answers, the discipline of psychology can help in answering such general questions as:

—How does the manager create an atmosphere in which competent people can grow?
—How does he define effectiveness and the results sought?
—How can he establish the motivational climate for people with different needs who have to motivate themselves to be productive?
—How does he recognize and reward performance?
—How does he reconcile individual needs with the demands of the organization?
—How does he account for a person performing brilliantly in one set of circumstances and dismally in others?

Answers to these and other questions of productivity and achievement are difficult in any business. They are becoming more difficult in the era of knowledge work which depends on the contributions of professional specialists.

Ordinarily most people would think that measuring the achievements of a salesman would be the easiest of all business functions. But even for salesmen, defining effectiveness is a difficult task that must be thought through rigorously. All types of responses are possible. Is he being measured by total sales volume? If so, is the target in terms of dollars, physical units, number of units, product line, quotas, previous year's sales, average sales per call, new customer sales, percentage of sales to calls, number of accounts lost, profit contributions, potential of the sales territory, ability to hold accounts and generate new sales? Or is it a combination of several of the above standards; if so, what weight is given to each category? All of these factors will have elements of motivation, but first the job expectations and results must be defined. The deeper one probes the more difficult it is to give precise answers, but judgments must be made in identifying contributions. If the job of defining effectiveness is difficult for a salesman, it is even more complicated for a cost accountant, systems analyst, research scientist or a quality control engineer.

CHAPTER VI

The Entrepreneurial Executive

INTRODUCTION

Over a generation ago, James H. Stauss, Professor of Economics, University of Tennessee, provided us with an insightful clue for enlarging the entrepreneurial role of executives when he asserted that "the entrepreneur is the firm."[1] Because human resources are crucial for improving performance and implementing opportunities, it is implicit in Stauss' assumption that the locus of entrepreneurship cannot reside exclusively with top management. The enterprise requires an entrepreneurial ethos from all knowledge executives contributing to corporate goals. Top management under conditions of risk and uncertainty will continue to formulate strategic objectives shaping the mission of the firm, but on other levels knowledge professionals will also encounter risk and uncertainty in their tasks of implementation. In short, because the entrepreneurial function is synonymous with the management of change, an entrepreneurial spirit in which administration is supplemented with a focus on performance and opportunities, should permeate all layers of the organization.

To meet the growing needs of society in the last quarter of the century, today's large business organizations face the challenge of developing entrepreneurial executives. The task of inculcating an entrepreneurial outlook will entail two major requirements: managerial literacy and managing knowledge work.

Managerial Literacy

The traditional path of achieving top management status in American business was for an executive to display competency in this specialty during the early stages of his career. After scaling the rungs of the ladder to the heights of top management, the executive was then expected to develop the talent of a generalist by simultaneously comprehending the entire business and unlearning his specialty. In this respect the practice of business has been at variance with the older professions of law, medicine, theology, and teaching, all of which emphasized generalist training initially and the branching out into a specialty subsequently. The time appears right for business to emulate, at least in part, the approach of the older professions.

The entrepreneurial process is incompatible with the narrow functional business approach. Specialized training fails to clarify corporate identity, the basic understanding of what the business is and what it should become. Waiting until an executive enters the upper levels of top management before being exposed to an integrated generalist approach is both dangerous and costly. Moreover, it may be too late in one's career to develop a broader entrepreneurial vision. At the same time, the answer is not in training generalists, *per se* which has serious shortcomings. There is a lot to be said for the moral requirement that every individual executive learn one discipline in depth. In addition entrepreneurship demands that the executive enlarge his professional competency by acquiring managerial literacy. In short, besides knowing how his own specialty contributes to corporate results, the entrepreneurial executive will have to develop a general knowledge of the other corporate survival functions. Managerial literacy does not call for an individual to be an expert in other fields but demands an understanding of how other disciplines contribute to one's own field, and how one's own knowledge contributes to other functional specialities.

Managing Knowledge Work

Knowledge, or mental capital, is currently the major cost center of every large business. Entrepreneurial executives must face the reality of managing a knowledge organization. In post-industrial society the emphasis will be less and less on craft and experience and more and more on translating concepts and ideas into economic results.

The traditional business organization is patterned on military and ecclesiastical models, emphasizing apprenticeship and experience. The organizational chart of formal organizations also implies top management omniscience which is a myth. It is impossible for a single top man, or a group of men, to comprehend the countless knowledge disciplines necessary to run a large organization. The reality of knowledge work dictates that the old fashioned organization chart will diminish in importance. For a variety of reasons the organizational chart will not disappear, but the vertical features of scalar organization will be replaced with matrix characteristics of interaction. Status is being substituted by knowledge as the real authority in the modern corporation. In the knowledge organization, professionals who are obscured in the organizational chart are often making vital business decisions. To cite just one example, on the occasion of a business undertaking a crucial merger decision, the key to the commitment will be the tax specialist. Yet, when one tries to locate his position in the organizational structure, it is almost impossible to find him.

In the typical pattern of corporate decision making, management scientists, financial analysts, lawyers, accountants, tax specialists, market research experts, research scientists, personnel people, along with a host of outside consultants attached to the system, depending upon the specific situation, will be called upon for input. Because they have the authority of knowledge and control crucial elements of information, they are, in effect, making risk taking entrepreneurial commitments. Isolated functional decisions are dangerous, if they are not interrelated with the business mission.

The reality of task or matrix management means that the traditional focus of supervising subordinates will have diminished significance in knowledge work. The real areas of contribution for the entrepreneurial executive will be lateral and upward. In short, how does he make a knowledge contribution to his peers and his boss? It will be impossible for entrepreneurial executives to be effective unless the spirit of entrepreneurship, with its pursuit of opportunities and improved professional performance, permeates all levels of the organization. Instead of proclaiming a false omniscience, the fostering of the entrepreneurial spirit will increasingly become a major objective of top management.

Positioning For Entrepreneurial Effectiveness

The disagreements and contradictions among the academic theorists, the satirical slashes of the guerrilla writers, and the alleged infallibility of the hard nosed skeptics, mentioned in the previous chapter, have failed to provide "an operational code" for executive effectiveness. Indeed, aside from the important factor of understanding one's self, the objective observer will have difficulty finding a single absolute operational law for all organizations and occasions in the conventional wisdom of the literature.

Different approaches to the problem of executive and entrepreneurial effectiveness are needed. In searching for deeper understanding, the approach should be on the dynamics of the business enterprise, focusing on two main themes: managerial literacy centering on the strategic theory of the firm and the operating milieu of managerial work. Understanding the background of these two themes may then make it possible to weave the insights of the theorists into a more meaningful fabric. Moreover, without an organizing focus, the isolated approach of behavioral principles will operate in a vacuum. In order for executives at every level of the organization to manage change more effectively, an entrepreneurial approach encompassing a deeper understanding of corporate realities and the application of pragmatic guidelines is required.

The Strategy Stance

In *Strategy and Structure*,[2] Alfred D. Chandler, Professor of Business History, Harvard Business School, presents a brilliant clinical study of several of our leading businesses, stressing the point that the emphasis on structure has been misplaced. He states that the tactic of other companies borrowing the organizational styles and forms of successful corporate institutions such as General Motors, Sears Roebuck, DuPont, and Standard Oil is improbable and is the equivalent of putting the organizational cart before the strategic horse. Without a coherent and lucid set of objectives, the grafting of an organization framework is a futile exercise. According to Chandler, strategy should always shape structure.

We have learned that when brilliant men move into new settings, such as into other businesses or into the government, they are often unable to make successful contributions. To say that a good "General Electric man" will make a good "Sears Roebuck man" may be on the surface a convincing statement, but the odds are against the probability of a successful transition. In short, instead of affirming that a manager can potentially manage any business, there is a good deal to the argument of having a feel for an industry and knowing one business in depth.

Recent research by students of the multinational corporation has revealed that it is no easy task to transfer individual executive styles to a different set of objectives in an alien setting and different value system. Objectives and managerial operating codes must adjust to the environment and not the other way around. The conclusion should not be made that organization is unimportant; but, the structural skeleton is residual to the substantive strategy which is based on the unique knowledge of the business and understanding the needs of the customer. Structure is a means of implementing the strategy; but, without a clear mental picture of the business' identity, the organizational chart becomes a sham.

Unfortunately, from the point of view of executive and entrepreneurial performance, one of the great difficulties in implementing objectives for any large organization is that people see the structure but are only dimly aware of the strategy. They are all too familiar with the neat scheme of organizational charts and the pious platitudes of job description, but neither has much direct relationship in contributing toward total business result. The startling remoteness in understanding business objectives for most executives and professionals is fairly easy to document. Executives are proficient in describing their specialized functional work in the immediate job setting, but vagueness and ambivalence prevail when questioned about key entrepreneurial questions such as:

—What is your business?
—What will the business be in the next five years?
—What should the business be?
—What are the central knowledge excellencies?
—Who is the customer?
—What are the channels of distribution?
—Who are the non-customers?
—Who is the non-competition?
—What is the real knowledge that the customer pays for?
—What does the customer consider value?

Responses to these entrepreneurial questions often evoke blank stares or parroting of unsophisticated answers from the annual stockholder report. Of course, the answers will vary widely with the organization and individual. Often these questions are unfair because top management has failed to think them through. In those instances where there is no unified vision, the confusion is only more pronounced. But even in those cases where top management has profoundly thought through objectives there is little evidence in most businesses that they have been communicated downward. Executives throughout the organization, feeling they have little accountability for entrepreneurial thinking, go randomly about performing their functional tasks.

The fact is, however, they do the important entrepreneurial work or implementation and most of it hinges on the strategic decisions which have been consciously or unconsciously hidden from them.

Internal structure blocks the larger strategic vision with the result that entrepreneurial effectiveness is enervated. The business as a whole is the unit of total results. Everything else is a cost center and by itself totally useless. In failing to see the real commitments and the mission of the company, we could easily get the impression that many executives could just as well have been working for some non-profit making organization. The entrepreneurial decisions of risk and opportunity, the life blood of any business in a period of radical change, elude the majority of management practitioners. Without an entrepreneurial understanding of business objectives the outcome is bureaucratic drift resulting in over administration and undermanagement, a certain prescription for ineffectiveness.

Consequently, the starting point for managerial and entrepreneurial effectiveness depends on understanding the objectives of the business. Objectives hinge on the responses to many of the previously mentioned strategic questions. Stated bluntly, they boil down to whether or not what executives are doing makes sense in terms of our customers and knowledge. And does what they do make sense in terms of tomorrow. It is not imperative that everybody agree with the strategic value judgments, but it is crucial for all professionals with responsibility to understand them. Without an understanding of objectives, communications deteriorate into status; functional divisions erect their various empires; symbols of status and rank precede achievement and accomplishment; and the breach between the perceptual logic of the individual and the organization leads to greater confusion. Management is the bringing together of many different knowledges for joint performances; organization is the tool for achieving this end. Focusing on objectives provides an escape from internal organizational myopia in understanding outside opportunities, and equally important, it promotes awareness in the thinking part of managerial work by assuming the work can be organized and systematized into operating guidelines for business results.

"Where there is no vision," King Solomon proclaimed, "people will perish." Clear goals energize the organization by providing the dynamics for achievement. When functionalism and specialization prevail there is an accompanying low level of performance and a loss of commitment. When everybody becomes a pursuer of his specialty, business skills take precedence over managerial and entrepreneurial skills. For example, personnel people in looking only at interpersonal relations and job descriptions would not be found reading an income statement. Accountants rarely read anything else given their passion for the bottom line of profit and loss statements. Production people see turning out goods as the prime desideratum, thinking it unfashionable to worry about costs and materials. Computer people wallow in problem solving, but are often indifferent to whether the problems are relevant to corporate results. Research scientists find curious delight in investigating frontier problems of knowledge which they find personally interesting but ignore business opportunities based on the knowledge foundation of the company. Engineers want to probe what is difficult, while often ignoring the needs of the customer. Sales people think that more and more volume will solve every problem in the business. Pursuit of function alone produces in all professional specialists a condition of managerial illiteracy.

On the other hand, all successful organizations have one central common denominator. Their chief advantage over mediocre companies is their ability to define themselves with a reasonably clear vision and communicate their sense of economic mission to professionals in the organization. As a result professionals in successful organizations have a conceptual grasp of managerial literacy. In making the metamorphosis toward managerial literacy, effective executives recognize that there will be turbulence and conflict among the various specialists, that it is possible to only learn one specialty in depth, that it is necessary to understand not the skills but the fundamentals of other disciplines, and that the goal is to have the specialized function make a contribution to the entire business.

The Managerial Climate

Although the communication of reasonably clear objectives throughout the organization is the starting point of executive effectiveness, by themselves, objectives are no guarantee of performance. The implementation of company objectives requires clearly focused work. This is not necessarily the same as hard work. In the final analysis, the customer is not especially interested in how diligently people are working. In terms of results, there is probably a low correlation between excessive effort and ineffectiveness. A sure sign of misallocation is doing those things efficiently which should not be done at all. Unfortunately, the organizational climate of large organizations is deficient in the nourishment of managerial and entrepreneurial work.

Brilliant managerial performance with an entrepreneurial focus is the exception; in the main, executive incompetence is in universal supply throughout large organizations. Incompetency is not synonomous with stupidity; the preponderance of professionals in business organizations are intellectually superior. However, because large organizations are inherently programmed for ineffectiveness, there is a glaring gap between potential and contribution. Poor performance is not usually the result of weak leadership at the top, although it may be a factor; nor, is it the result of apathy below, although this may also be a symptom. Incompetency is a result of the structural pathologies emanating from countless procedures, policies and regulations which had the initial intention of coordination and control but quickly degenerated into bureaucratic inertia.

The larger the organization the greater the internal procedures for stability and control, but these efforts are in vain given the input of external forces creating increased vulnerability upon the structure. Resolving the dilemma of dynamic organizational stability in the midst of radical change is a difficult task. It will not vanish by top management fiat, nor will it go away by good intensions from below; it is a reality that must be faced. Within the framework of this dilemma, there are entrenched obstacles to effectiveness confronting all levels of management. The common denominators deterring effective performance are only a question of degree with regard to the power of top or lower management. Without a clear understanding of these omnipresent barriers to effectiveness in the managerial milieu, there is little possible way of neutralizing them in the quest for greater entrepreneurial effectiveness. In short, if we seek improved executive performance it must initially emerge from the present operating climate; any other alternative would be quixotic, a point neglected by too many organizational and behavioral theorists.

In the academic treatment of executive effectiveness, the dominant emphasis has been on the characteristics of man's behavior with scant attention to the phenomenon of work. Nobody would deny the importance of the behavioral sciences, but studying the nature of executive work through the discipline of psychology alone is like performing an autopsy without a body. The fact that we know little about the concept of knowledge work probably accounts for the neglect and the tendency to take it for granted, but this hardly excuses the failure to bring what little we do know into focus. Executive effectiveness demands that the starting point be an understanding of professional work.

Among the most significant realities confronting all executives in their corporate work, four stand out sharply: the activist feature, the non-soloist dimension, the time factor, and the information and communication network.[3]

The Activist Feature

Nothing is impossible for the man who does not have to do it himself. Many of the assumptions contained in books about executive effectiveness neglect this aphorism. But the reality of executive work is continual activity, involving incessant doing. In the hectic atmosphere where events never stand still, there are always inevitable pressures to meet deadlines, prepare reports, produce quotas and to maintain the organization as an ongoing viable concern. Any management neglecting the needs of the customer and the test of profitability will not be around very long. The incessant demands of managerial work clearly separate it from the meditating role of the philosopher. In general, idealism usually increases in direct proportion to one's distance from the problem.

At the same time the burden of accomplishing the immediate is so distracting that executives push the thinking part of the job in any systematic or organized fashion into the background. In the nature of things, doing takes precedence over thinking. Many may argue intellectually that this is too big a price to pay, but the stress on incessant activity will not evaporate of its own accord.

The demands of doing are further complicated by the entrepreneurial characteristic of uncertainty. Moreover, crises are uncongenial to the principles listed in the behavioral and organization textbooks. There is always the pervasive reality of Murphy's Law, namely "that everything that can go wrong will go wrong." There is also its corollary that inevitably once a job is fouled up, everything done to improve it makes it worse. In the encounter with uncertainties and crises, "putting out fires" is the normal pattern of the day, with little thought to the element of prevention. The focus on doing becomes even more exacerbated when people causing the confusion are sometimes rewarded for superior performance after taking credit for extinguishing their conflagrations.

Ideally, the well-managed company is unexciting and undramatic, which is the exception. The manager responsible for immediate performance sees confusion roughly organized in his daily activities and takes a dim view of academic and theoretical principles in such an atmosphere. President Harry Truman's remark that: "If you can't stand the heat you better get out of the kitchen" is a candid reminder that the executive job is no sinecure.

The alert executive must be constantly aware of the pitfalls of the activity trap. The inevitable result of devoting excessive attention to controls leads to loss of control of resources; undue attention to prevention of waste dilutes the entrepreneurial function; rigorous emphasis on costs alone tends to obscure opportunities; devotion to doing things right often prevents doing the right things; and administrative activity alone without contribution and achievement erodes the foundation of motivation.

The Non-Soloist Dimension

The doctor in his office, the artist at his easel, the teacher in the classroom, the lawyer preparing his brief, the novelist at his typewriter are all examples of isolated professional work in which the guidelines of accountability and responsibility for results are clearly delineated. In the corporate universe of interdependence, the soloist function is virtually non-existent. Of necessity, the executive must get things done through people.

Everybody in the organization, including top management, manages and is managed simultaneously. Top management has only a vague idea of the countless disciplines required to run a modern organization. Although it may exercise veto power, it must rely on the knowledge professionals for its decision making. Highly intricate task work involving many disciplines modifies the status and rank position of the scalar organizational chart. At the same time within the task configuration of the informal group structure, it is almost impossible to identify the individual contribution of the various specialists. There is no concrete evidence that professional specialists (cost accountants, market research staff, or quality control engineers) contribute anything directly to the product, yet they are indispensable to total business performance. The only result we are sure of in the cross-fertilization of business talents is that the whole is greater than the sum of its parts; in this sense it is remote from any traditional soloist function.

It is the job of the expert in a large organization to make himself understood and not operate on the assumption that others learn his discipline. It is only when the individual relates his specialty to his peers and superiors that his knowledge becomes relevant for business results. Invariably, this entails conflict among differing temperaments, different knowledge backgrounds and diverse value systems, making the job of management more complex. It is wishful thinking to expect engineers, salesmen, or accountants to stop fighting; the company will be in real trouble if they do stop. However, when the group tensions are transcended in common effort the results are infinitely greater than the individual working alone, but the process is never a smooth one and is filled with all varieties of friction and turbulence.

The Time Factor

Time is the dominant resource of individuals and organizations; but for executives, time is not their own, they are captives of time. In the corporate pattern of mutual interdependence, time does not belong to the individual; the organizational relationships stake out prior claims.

Countless intrusions on available time pose the skeptical question of how any work gets done at all, and the larger the organization the greater the amount of interruptions. Committees and meetings serve as a case in point. Unnecessary meetings and abundance of committees have served as the basis of numerous jokes ridiculing the executive scene. Among some of the most frequently listed barbs about committees forming an inchoate folklore are the following:

— A group of the unwilling, appointed by the unfit, to do the unnecessary.
— A committee of three gets things done if two don't show up.
— A group of men who individually can do nothing, but as a group meet and decide that nothing can be done.
— A body that keeps minutes and wastes hours.
— The confusion of the loudest talking character multiplied by the number of those present.
— If you want to kill any idea, get a committee to work on it.
— The ultimate in meetings: a meeting to call a meeting.

Everybody complains meekly about the monstrous cluttering of meetings interfering with work, but at the same time, everybody passively accepts them as an irrevocable part of corporate life. Excessive meetings are a certain sign of bureaucratic pathology and failure in communications. There is no observable evidence that meetings produce meaningful work results. Properly used, meetings have their place in setting an agenda for future work, seeing that various alternatives are explored, establishing constructive conflict and assisting the development of effective communications and relationships; but productive work *per se* does not take place in meetings. Moreover, they can become detriments in stealing time away from important work tasks.

Committees and meetings are not the only time scavengers. Time availability depends on numerous relationships throughout the organization; the executive must constantly react to other people's plans, priorities, and activities. In the typical pattern of work, the executive provides information for his peers, serves the demands of his superiors, wrestles with the problems of subordinates, reacts with a Pavlovian predictability to the rings of the telephone, listens to complaints of customers, and struggles with deadlines. All these represent a small portion of the demands on his time and none can be neglected except at great peril to his career. There is little evidence, however, that any of these features can be automatically eliminated; they are realities of organizational work. If the executive attempts to isolate himself in too drastic a fashion, he becomes ineffective. On the other hand, if his door is always open, the demands on his time increase exponentially. The real problem for management is to obtain a meaningful perspective on the reality of what is actually happening in the corporate universe. The penchant of people wanting things, the demands on time, the predigestion of all information, and the need to make continuing survival decisions all contribute to making the manager's job increasingly difficult. Although every manager must resolve the dilemma of time according to his talents and temperament, there is little question that he needs bigger blocks of disposable time in order to become more effective.

The Information and Communication System

With the torrents of trivia and the deluge of data, no executive can escape the flood of the company's information system. And the larger the organization, the more he is confined to the inundation of rules, regulations, policies and procedures. Once typewriter reports were required in duplicate, but with Xerox the proliferation of reports stagger even the speed reading capacity of the recipients. Tidal waves of paper have multiplied the factor of handling, which by definition is waste, barren of results, and a degenerative aspect of managerial work. Executives contribute to the problem by drowning their colleagues in a stream of memos. Moreover, the merciless time demands always exceed time availability in plowing through the swamp of paperwork. Unless countered in some positive fashion, it drains away discretionary time for the thinking part of the job in seeking new opportunities. The great danger is that unless the executive systematically charts a course toward disposable time he will drift aimlessly with the rest of the flotsam and jetsam in the bureaucratic sea.

As the executive ascends the heights of the management ladder, the time dilemmas become increasingly acute. And for top management, the brain function of the business, the pressures are inordinately demanding. It is because of the unimaginable tensions and enormous responsibilities of top management that the need for disposable time is even more important. Consider briefly the items demanding the attention of a top manager on a given day. A cursory look at his calendar would reveal the following: meeting with top level colleagues from his own industry, confrontation with a consumer group, session with a key government regulator, a visit from a college president requesting money, conference with his leading executives on new product strategy, visit from a labor leader, sandwiched telephone calls from prominent customers, interview with a reporter on social responsibility and compulsory attendance on the banquet circuit. In almost every instance cited above, the individuals contacting him want something from him. They will frequently embroider the truth, not because they are maliciously trying to take advantage of him, but because they frequently need his support for their activities.

There is an identifiable correlation between increased size and the communication process. As Julian Huxley, the English biologist, remarked: "Simply magnify an object, without changing its shape, and meaning to, you have changed all its properties."[4] From the research of the biologist, D'Arcy Thompson, we know that the surface of an object increases with the square of the diameter, and the mass with the diameter's cube. For example as the diameter goes from 2 to 3 to 4, the mass expands from 8 to 27 to 84, while the surface increases only from 4 to 9 to 16.[5] From a managerial point of view if the concept is pushed to the ultimate, we encounter the analogy of the dinosaur and the brain. Moreover, any network system displays diseconomies of scale if expansion is allowed to go on unabated. The number of things connected in any switching formula is characterized by the function of

$$\frac{N \times (N-1)}{2},$$

which results essentially in a square.[6] In short, the additional extension of one unit to an organization does not simply mean adding another single factor, but involves the quantitative growth in relationships of approximately a square.

In large organizations, there is no evidence that the exponential increase in information has improved the communication process. Systematized ignorance is still ignorance. Indeed, the opposite corollary prevails: the greater the information, the less communication. There is a physical limit to any individual's information absorption, and if he attempts to encompass too much, the result is a blur culminating in seeing nothing.

From the standpoint of entrepreneurial effectiveness (*i.e.*, focusing on opportunities resulting in business contribution), the information pattern evokes an inexorable drift toward misallocation of resources placing emphasis on problems rather than opportunities, stressing efficiency at the expense of effectiveness, attending to frictions instead of results, seeing the urgent and not the important and directing energies toward the past rather than the future. In short, most information contributes to red ink.

The Quest for Entrepreneurial Effectiveness

The aforementioned realities help explain why effective executives are such unbelievably rare commodities and why mediocrity is the rule rather than the exception. Affirming the realities promoting ineffectiveness, however, does not mean that nothing can be done to modify the obstacles connected with corporate work. The quest for entrepreneurial effectiveness assumes that although few are attaining the dividends inherent in their potential, it also infers that everybody is capable of improvement and change through organized and systematic effort. In frankly recognizing that the impediments to performance cannot be erased, this does not mean that by a calculated personal thrust it is not possible to neutralize them. In introducing systematized thought and effort into the pattern of confusion roughly organized, misallocation of resources can be curbed and the focus on entrepreneurial performance enhanced.

In the search for converting the problem into an opportunity, a number of guidelines forming the foundation for an entrepreneurial operational code emerge: contribution, concentration, awareness of time, the element of strength, the discipline of practice, and the vision of professional commitment.

Contribution

Raising the question of contribution involves for a professional or an executive the justification of his paycheck, and the higher the rank and emoluments the greater the need for justification. The question infers that every corporate professional is a high grade resource, making it necessary to inquire of himself whether the company is receiving appropriate value in return for his services.

In this regard, the definition of a professional executive has two basic dimensions—the objective and the subjective. The former involves status and rank in the hierarchical chart; the higher the position the

The Entrepreneurial Executive

greater the expected impact within the organization. The latter executive definition embraces psychological connotations; it includes everybody regardless of rank, who considers himself responsible for concrete contributions and rejects the perceptual view of himself as a subordinate. Consequently, the subjective definition is far more inclusive and widens the arena of entrepreneurial responsibility.

On the other hand, the objective definition with its focus on titles, the genuflection is to job descriptions which often reflect past realities and prior performance expectations. The assumption of literal job descriptions can be seriously challenged in the modern world of knowledge work and the management of change. Most job descriptions deal with statements about activity rather than with opportunities and contributions to business performance. Regardless of its title and emolument, no job has any descriptive future; the future is made by the man and not the position. Most of the people who qualify for executive positions concentrate on the objective factors; in doing so they become candidates for bureaucratic puppetry. Those who take the psychological definition have opened the door toward entrepreneurial effectiveness.

In specific terms, the executive who undertakes the subjective definition must come to grips with the question: What is my job? In thinking through this thorny question of meaningful entrepreneurial contribution, it is unlikely that the answer will be the same as his objective job description. In general, his place within the organizational chart will usually dictate activities conducive to misallocations of his talent and contributions. It usually spells out the vectors of his routine administrative functions. The job description does not meet the challenge of what results are needed to do a superb job: the areas of real accountability and responsibility, the central core of the contribution to the enterprise. A penetrating probing for the nucleus of the job center forces the individual to think through those priority areas of meaningful contribution that he alone is capable of making, and conceivably concluding that those things which do not fit may be somebody else's job. The analysis of a job center is not the same as delegation which too frequently masquerades as "buck passing." Indeed, when an executive assumes he is responsible for his own results, much of what is labeled under the rubric of delegation disappears.

Focusing on contribution calls attention to the fact that knowledge is becoming the reigning authority in executive work and rules out using specialized knowledge as a crutch for misdirected performance. Hiding behind the academic jargon of one's specialty obscures rather than promotes contribution. Experts have a penchant for talking about something they do not understand and making you think it is your fault. The secret of professional performance entails making one's specialization understood to those requiring this knowledge for their own contribution to the organization.

The lines and vectors of the organization chart suggest that superiors direct subordinates; however, much of supervisory mentality dissolves in the application of knowledge work to business opportunities. When this reality is fully recognized, the role a knowledge professional as a subordinate loses most of its traditional meaning. Therefore, instead of assuming that we can manage others, the authority of knowledge maintains the only person one can really manage is oneself. One cannot learn from other people's experience, one can learn only from one's own.

Managing others, a relic of old military and scalar organizational forms, but in a knowledge organization, it is a specie of arrogance, probably imprudent, possibly immoral and conducive to sabotage from below. The best that one can hope for in dealing with professional subordinates is the projection of objectives, making sure you are not your subordinate's problem by interfering with his work, communicating instructions clearly, providing a good example, setting high standards and creating a sound atmosphere where good people can grow and make a contribution. Most of the literature on training and supervision are residues of the old craft technology with its emphasis on quantitative production norms. It has little or no relevance for knowledge work where the emphasis is on qualitative contribution for accountable results. As mentioned earlier, the goal of changing personalities advanced by certain behaviorists is also self-defeating. But through mutual respect and joint endeavor, a superior can help draw out the talent of subordinates for substantive results.

Textbooks on organizations continue to place undue emphasis on the span of control principle, which fosters manipulation and a downward orientation. The span of control doctrine with its excessive levels leads to an erosion of managerial performance and a dilution of the entrepreneurial spirit by impeding contribution and stifling initiative. It is not the levels of organization and the number of people reporting to an executive that dictate contribution. It is not the descriptive relevance of the span of control but the operating reality of span of relationship (*i.e.*, the number of people the executive has to work with for results) that counts.[7]

Task work, the key activity of modern organizational life, dictates cooperation and interaction with others. Consequently, the real payoff is lateral (requirements of peers) and upward (needs of superior) in making a contribution to the organization. Too often the boss is seen as the obstacle to progress; this is usually an unreasonable assumption since he probably would not have arrived where he is without some talent. More often than not, friction with the boss results from a communication gap caused by differing perceptual realities. The fact remains, however, unless the individual can make a contribution toward the success of his superior, chances are that he will also fail. In order to avoid the boss failing, an intelligent effort must be made to understand his perception of reality, adjust to his managerial style, recognize his strengths and identify his needs.

In summary, the focus on contribution means the recognition that the professional worker is a higher level asset; that he concentrates on his job center; that he focuses on contribution rather than effort *per se*; that he is only sure of managing himself, that the downward thrust is conducive to friction and not results; and that the real contribution emanates from a lateral and upward focus.

Concentration

Warning against the wide dispersal of talent, the pre-Socratic Greek philosopher, Democritus, remarked: "Do not try to understand everything or you will be ignorant of everything."[8] The wisdom of this dictum becomes immediately apparent with a cursory examination of great models of leadership. Almost without exception their high levels of attainment rested on the iron law of concentration. Able people avoid spreading themselves too thin by recognizing it is better to do less, competently, than more, poorly. Consequently, in determining where efforts should be concentrated, they achieve optimal results with minimum effort.

Effective people also have the capacity of seeking out their excellencies through a priority system of planning. In the search for concentration, however, posteriorities (what we leave out) is equally important as the priorities. Newton's law of physics states that for every action there is a reaction; similarly, as an administrative principle, every priority must have its anti-priority or posteriority. Omissions may have deeper impact on executive performance than a general statement of priority objectives. Without a tradeoff on goals, there is the human tendency to plan to do too much with the result that the individual may be overwhelmed by a profusion of key priorities. It is a rarity to find a manager who does not have more ideas than he knows how to handle adequately. The normal temptation is to compromise and do a little bit of everything. Trying to accomplish too much is a certain formula for ineffectiveness. On the other hand, emphasizing posteriorities helps assure that the proper things will be sought out and less time will be wasted. Finally, the focus on posteriorities promotes an acute awareness that we are being paid not for efforts but for results.

The key to concentration is the principle of abandonment. In executive work there is a quagmire syndrome which fosters the tendency of adding to tasks, but rarely giving anything up. Northcote C. Parkinson is correct in asserting that work tends to expand to fill available time. Consequently, executives often spend dollar time on penny jobs that should not be done at all. One of the worse sins against managerial performance is the inclination to do a little more efficiently, those things which should not be done at all.

Factoring in abandonment and attaining concentration are difficult tasks, which are not easily resolved by statements of description. They require profound probing in the nature of executive contribution. Planning by questions may be a useful analytical tool:

—What are the things that cease to be productive?
—What one important thing do you want to do tomorrow, and what one ineffective thing do you want to stop doing today?
—If I had a choice and were not doing it today, should I really be doing it?
—Should I candidly admit that the things I am postponing I am really abandoning?
—What would happen if somebody else took care of it?
—What risks would I take if I did nothing at all?
—In my professional routine, do I have a pattern for distinguishing the urgent from the important, the past from the future and the efficient from the effective?
—After appropriate discussion with my superior, what is the one agreed upon priority that I want to try to accomplish within the next six months which will have a qualitative impact on the company?

Awareness of Time

Without question time is our most precious resource and also the one most wasted. A company can hire people, but it can never rent time. It is unpurchasable, perishable, unstorable and irreversible; once it passes it is uncapturable. Horace Mann, the eminent American educator, summarized this point when, for his amusement, he inserted an advertisement into the columns of a local newspaper, which read:

> Lost, yesterday, somewhere between sunrise and sunset, two golden hours, each studded with sixty diamond units. No reward offered, they are gone forever.[9]

Throughout history, the subject of time has been an intellectual challenge for countless philosophers. Perhaps no one has captured its clusive and ephemeral spirit more than St. Augustine. In Book XI of his famous *Confessions*, he reminds us that past time is nothing but fragile and distorted memory, that future time is a form of premeditation and that only present time has perceptual meaning. St. Augustine asserts: "Time can only be perceived or measured while it is passing."[10] Moreover, he provides us with the brilliant insight that there are no facts in the future, there are only expectations. With regard to this comment, he writes:

> Future things then are not as yet: and if they be not yet, they are not: and if they are not, they cannot be seen; yet foretold they may be from things present, which are already, and can be seen.[11]

Because we live in a state of duration we tend to underestimate time's elusive quality. According to Murphy's third law, everything takes longer than you think. Nobody ever has enough time; yet, paradoxically, everybody has all there is. It is the one executive resource that is distributed equally to all. In concentrating on the linear features of time with its quantitative feature of minutes, hours and days, most people misuse their time in taking a random walk through life. As a result of faulty perception, the qualitative factors of time relationships are neglected. A tendency exists for the manager to misdiagnose where time is and should be going compared to the reality of where it actually goes. Moreover, since people have different qualitative time perceptions, telling people how to manage time by prescription is like King Canute trying to stop the ocean waves. Nevertheless, unless executives are not to fall victims of the drift of time, they have a responsibility in curbing the restrictive forces of organizational life and seeking the dividends of disposal time for contributions and results.

It is paradoxical but true that the people who have apparently the least time are usually also the most productive. By being more productive they are able to blunt the negative factors creating a loss of time and energy. Improved output is related to refinement of technique in the management of time. These executives realize that the time spent on planning saves time in implementation.

The philosopher Schopenhauer once wrote: "Ordinary people think merely how to spend time, a man of talent tries to use it." The first step in the improved utilization is the recognition that time demands will always exceed time resources. Given this inescapable reality, the first general rule in handling time is knowing how it is presently allocated. Since reliance on memory is too amorphous, the wise executive will use the simple tools of pencil and paper and keep a running record. At the same time a time check should stimulate a person to get rid of unproductive efforts.

The approach of doing many things at once is an invitation to inefficiency and a misuse of time. Using time constructively requires doing only one important thing at a time. Brief spurts of time directed towards crucial problems will not produce results; important things cannot be done in periods of short duration. If a person is responsible for a key position paper, a major presentation or a difficult human relation problem, he needs large blocks of time to achieve meaningful performance. Brief time spans may serve as a profitable refresher and review subsequent to concentrated investment of time, but the commitment of large units of time is crucial for priority affairs. With important assignments, we should write down what one expects to happen. As a form of internal communication in thinking through the problem, it is a form of feedback and will save time in the long run.

Skillful use of time demands insights of personal self knowledge. People have different temperaments and energy levels. Some are more competent as early risers, others work better at night. Some operate better under heavy pressure, others require a more leisurely tempo. Some perform better in isolation, others are more effective in groups. Some communicate better orally, others by writing. Some perform more competently with a great deal of sleep, others adjust to shorter periods of rest. The combinations and permutations are as infinite as there are individuals, for the effective use of time each executive must diagnose his own pattern of self control.

However, research from the models of successful executives suggest some broad common denominators for the effective mastery of time. No universal list is possible, but the following may be helpful:

—Enumerate goals for the day in terms of results, not activities.
—Avoid using what you consider the most productive part of the day

for procedural work. Allocate special periods of time for the consolidation of such routines as mail, newspaper, correspondence, telephone, etc.
—Come to the office a half hour early, so you can plan the day in a fresh manner and concentrate without interference. It is not a question of managing the clock as much as managing oneself.
—Start meetings and appointments on time, it provides one with the feeling that he is in better control of the situation.
—Acknowledge that all handling is waste and make a concerted effort never to handle a piece of paper more than once, if possible respond by answering on the original. Although there may be occasional risks, use the wastebasket as an important tool of disposal. Information should only be addressed to those people requiring it.
—Meetings are important vehicles of communication; however, they continue in direct proportion to the number of people attending. Therefore, try to avoid those meetings where you can make no contribution and do not invite people who have no need of the communication and do not have to be there. A guideline for limiting the number of people attending a meeting would be to make the assumption that each member invited will take up fifteen minutes of time.
—Unintentionally or not, people are voracious time consumers, protect yourself against inordinate demands made upon you by cultivating polite and courteous tactics. It is amazing how many people refuse to say no for fear of being disliked.
—As a tool the telephone is neutral; it is senseless to blame its excessive use on the tool. On the one hand, it avoids meetings, saves useless trips, and cuts down on letter writing and paper work. On the other hand, it can be abused if it is allowed to intrude on your work and the work of others. It is wise to curtail calls and institute an organized callback system.
—Trusting one's memory is hazardous, write down what you expect to happen and hold results against expectations.
—Endeavor to read most books like a newspaper for key ideas, read only for the meaningful details. If it appears useful at some later date, keep a card index file on it.
—What do I have to learn today to keep renewing the learning process for tomorrow?
—Calculate the monetary worth of your time by the hour and consider return the same way as any other corporate investment.

—Apply the diagnostic technique with relation to problems. When you cannot find an answer, stop, and save time by redefining the problem.
—Plan for the unexpected, never plan for every minute of the day. Leave room for flexibility by setting aside some time for uninterrupted concentration.[12]

A more profound mastery of the management of time transcends personal temperaments and techniques, it involves a deeper probing of one's self-image and personal value system. Without a psychological awareness of the self-image in relationship to the environment, the approach to time will be gimmicky rather than substantive.

Procrastination

Because of its peculiarly enervating effects, procrastination merits special mention in any discussion of time. The propensity to talk about intentions and the proclivity to delay until ideal conditions prevail are afflictions confined to all but the most effective. Because it contributes to lost opportunities, increases pressures on deadlines and generates crises, procrastination is the single greatest thief of time.

As Shakespeare stated in the words of King Claudius in *Hamlet*: "That we would do, we should do, when we would."[13] To choose time is to save time, doing things immediately without delay is the single biggest time saver. The American poet, Robert Frost, remarked: "More people die from worry than they do from work simply because they worry too much about work." Moreover, one discovers that most of the things people worry about rarely happen, and meaningful constructive activity not only gives rest to the body but helps register peace of mind. In failing to get started, the things nagging at us take an increased psychological burden. Knowing what we are avoiding and admitting guilt is often the major step toward the completion of any unpleasant task. Since any job gets harder the more we put it off, the secret of performance is to start and do a little bit often; even the biggest jobs will soon be completed. Finally, in postponing to some non-existent ideal future date, we run the risk of missing out on an important opportunity. Such an approach assumes that tomorrow will always be the same as today.

Although procrastination has heavy psychological overtones, a well-tested technique used by executives for priority tasks is the application of the concepts of: definition, delegation and deadline. *Definition* of the problem is the real decision concerning what is relevant; *delega-*

tion designates the aspect of accountability to whom and responsibility for what of the problem; and the setting of a realistic *deadline* helps assure that the problem will transcend the realm of good intentions. Once the problem is clearly defined with proper designation of accountability and responsibility along with the feedback of deadlines, the process of saving time and achievement is on its take-off stage.

The Element of Strength
An oft repeated expression in the business world is "So and so is a good man." On its face value this is a vacuous statement which often loses its conviction unless one also asks, "Good for what?" To say that a person is either good or competent is too vague. There must be a referent; he must be good for something specifically. The prime element of organization is to determine functional division of labor for the tasks at hand. It is a myth to assume that a man is good at everything; it defies both the law of probability and biology. All talent is random. The sum total of ability for all individuals is basically the same but varies in distribution. La Rochefocauld, the French moralist, captured this point, when he stated:

> God has put differing talents in man as trees in Nature: and each has its own special characteristic and aspect. . . . The finest pear tree cannot produce the most ordinary apple and the most splendid talent cannot duplicate the effect of the homeliest skill.[14]

In managerial effectiveness, the focus on strength assumes that it is impossible to build on weaknesses, either one's own or others. If the strengths are present, it may be possible to neutralize the weaknesses, but that is the best anyone can do. One must search for his unique competency and build on this area of excellence. Invariably, we must recognize that with great strengths come concomitant weaknesses. In fact, the greater the strengths the greater the weaknesses. This principle is amply documented in the lives of all great men. The vain search for a man with no weaknesses is likely to end up with mediocrity: where there are no vices there are likely to be no virtues. In this regard, discovering traits as a clue to strength is also likely to be self-defeating.

Without exception, searching for key character traits invariably winds up with contradictions among the traits. The only trait incapable of being compromised is integrity, the visceral reaction of whether or not you trust a person. The emphasis on integrity cannot be stressed enough. Regardless of the performance of an individual, if he lacks character, the long run results will be destructive. People are willing to forget such human frailties as incompetence, mediocrity and bad habits, but if integrity is missing everything else becomes meaningless.

Selecting people for key positions demands the keenest judgment on the part of those charged with the responsibility. Given the uncertainty of executive work, no rule book exists that will predict how a person will perform. On the basis of their backgrounds we should have expected great results from Presidents John Quincy Adams and Herbert Hoover. In many respects both were remarkable men, but they failed to achieve in the presidency. On the other hand, Harry Truman and Abraham Lincoln had undistinguished political careers; few would have been impressed with their resumes.

Although no check-off list or testing method is inadequate, a number of guidelines may assist in making staffing judgments.

—Avoid the inclination of viewing the job as part of natural law. Jobs must be structured by tasks and not personality traits. There is no future in any job. The future lies in the man who holds the job. In this regard it is wise to ignore such irrelevant factors as age. Junior or senior is meaningful only with respect to performance. Also, personal preferences, dislikes, ancestry, color, attendance at preferred schools, etc., are cosmetic features in the staffing function—all are meaningless if the real strengths are present. Effective executives start out with what a man can do rather than slavishly adhering to the job description. They do not confuse style which is largely window dressing with intrinsic strengths. General George Marshall, perhaps the greatest model of staffing in American history, never confused pseudo-charisma with substance. He always raised the question of what a man could do, ignoring personal idiosyncracies. Although he was aware of weaknesses, he considered them less important if the real strengths were there. Throughout the decades of the nineteen twenties and thirties in keeping his black book on talented officers, he searched for excellence in one major area in examining such figures as Dwight D. Eisenhower, George Patton, Omar Bradley, along with scores of others.[15]

—Jobs have to be made demanding and big. Structuring jobs in terms of the immediate present and minimum performance is a weak approach. Some men have jobs with thirty years' experience. Actually they have repeated the same experience thirty times but they have not grown to meet tomorrow's challenges. When this occurs early in a man's career it quenches his enthusiasm. In staffing, there should always be a focus on tomorrow's job to provide a sense of renewal. This process involves unlearning as well as learning.

—In looking for the best in a man seek out the best in yourself. At the same time, in staffing people do not fear strong subordinates. Clarence Francis, former president of General Foods Corporation, claimed that when he hired people who were smarter than he was, it proved in the long run that he was smarter than they were.

—Jobs should be structured around the man and his expectations for results rather than literal job descriptions. Most appraisal forms are counter-productive in that they dwell on weaknesses at the expense of strengths. As presently constituted, many appraisal forms force the evaluator to be negative causing an irreparable breach in the communication network. Instead of becoming a constructive learning dialogue, the appraisal deteriorates as the appraiser becomes more and more guilty, and the employee becomes more and more defensive.

Appraisal procedures should eliminate the negative by concentrating on key positive questions, such as: "What has the man done well?"; "What is he likely to do well in the future?"; "What support does he require to do well?"; "If I had a son or a daughter would I want either of them to work for this individual?"[16] Appraisal should be a partnership searching for strengths among mature adults and bring out in the process guidance, support and protection in a reciprocal fashion for the growth of both the superior and subordinate.

—Any list depicting an open invitation to ineffectiveness in staffing would include the following major items: failure to put the best and strongest people where the big opportunities are; the placing of continued increments of more and more things on the back of a competent person (there will always be the straw that will break the camel's back); the pious hope that a good man will bolster a mediocrity (the marriage of a cripple with a healthy person rarely produces a wholesome offspring).

—It is instructive to remember that as a general principle, the distance between the excellent and the average is always constant. In this regard the intelligent thing is not to move the entire mass, but concentrate the emphasis on moving the elite. Once the performance of the best has been improved, the others will begin to narrow the gap. Whether in medicine, athletics or any other discipline, once the leadership sets the pace, it becomes remarkably easy for the rest to emulate. We have seen this in medicine with open heart surgery and other breakthroughs and in athletics with the four minute mile and countless other records.

The Discipline of Practice

Obtaining the proper breaks, receiving a good education, serving under a brilliant boss, working in an opportunity industry, and being in the right place at the right time, are just some of the factors indicating that all successful executives require their share of luck. On the other hand, no distinguished executive career has been the result of fortune alone. On this point, Stephen Leacock, the Canadian humorist and economist, said: "I am a great believer in luck, and the harder I work, the luckier I become." All successful executives have been able through self-discipline to neutralize the counterproductive preoccupations of organizational work and to implement the qualitative principles of contribution, concentration, the judicious use of time and the building upon strengths into a meaningful work pattern. The common denominator of all successful performance rests on the ability to put into practice the qualitative effective habits which are lacking among mediocre colleagues.

Excellence in any practice is deceptively simple. Brilliant professional athletes, musicians and entertainers have mastered the skills of their discipline to perfection; but among the truly outstanding, they will add their unique artistic style to the basic skills. What looks easy to the uninitiated eye took years of hard work and dedication before the attainment of mastery. Of course, certain minimum mental and physical capacities are necessary, but the crucial force in excellent performance is practice. Part of this mastery process is the inner passion that failure is impossible unless the person gives up striving in the achievement of his goal. Perhaps, this is the real key to motivation as well.

No practice is effective until it becomes a habit through drive and incessant effort. The more we learn the less we have to think about and, as a corollary the more time we have to think. An individual needs self-discipline as Plato stressed centuries ago. He cannot learn from other people's experiences. Practice is less a matter of natural endowment than a management of one's self through self control. The quest for effectiveness is less a matter of traits, personality, or what is frequently labeled leadership, but developing effective habits. The philosopher William James stated: "Habit is second nature. Habit is ten times nature." The Duke of Wellington exclaimed: ". . . The more details of our daily lives we can hand over to the effortless custody of automation, the more our higher powers will be set free for their proper work. There is no more miserable person than the one whom nothing is habitual but indecision."[17]

The realm of theory or the subject matter is far less important than the internalized self-discipline. Any practice is fundamentally unteachable, but it may be learnable. The mastery of any discipline assumes that any properly motivated individual with average abilities is capable of entrepreneurial achievement. Democritus recognized this insight centuries ago when he remarked: "More men become good through practice than by nature."[18] Successful accomplishments depend less on native intelligence, advanced degrees and personality traits than on ingrained habits of work. In general, there is a low correlation between academic brilliance and meaningful performance. One of the classic shortcomings of brilliant people with enormous indigenous potential is the inability to recognize that successful performance degenerates into hard work.

Translating practice into performance for business results will always be an uncertain endeavor. Even in baseball where batting, fielding and pitching skills are distinctly quantifiable, the probability of successfully selecting major league players remains amazingly small, as the failing parade of "bonus babies" strikingly indicate. As one moves up the hierarchy from mechanical to conceptual skills of management, the difficulties become even more acute. It is heavily documented that the promising Phi Beta Kappa of twenty-two often turns out to be a disappointment at the age of thirty, whereas the plodding "C" student with less brilliance often turns out to be the most successful.

Branch Rickey, the master architect of the St. Louis and Brooklyn baseball teams, addressed himself to this point when he stated that Eddie Stanky, his second baseman, could not hit, field or throw on nearly the level of other major league players, but he would rather have him play second base than any other man in baseball because he found ways of beating the other team. Rickey recognized that through the imponderables of motivation and practice Stanky had transcended his natural limitations to such a degree that his performance was unquestioned. Stanky, like most successful executives, not only worked harder, he also worked smarter.

Commitment

Commitment has less to do with knowledge than with the will to manage; has less to do with theoretical principles than with temperament; and has less to do with good skills than with enthusiasm for organized and systematic work. The job of a professional manager is no sinecure, it is pressure ridden and involves a sacrifice of family and privacy. The managers who are successful reap considerable monetary rewards and prestigious status, but these are the benefits of mercenaries rather than professionals.

Beyond the financial remuneration is the more important commitment that he is doing something worthwhile, requiring supreme concentration and dedication. And with my suggested guidelines, it is never easy. Finally, managerial commitment means change. The executive must come to terms with his own identity, and leaving the familiar for the turbulent now requires continuing maturity. Vail, Alfred E. Sloan, Wood, among other great executive models, all had this intangible ingredient of commitment. In this sense the job is not for everybody; the job of leadership resists democratization. If an art ever gets popular, it ceases to be creative; professional artists will always be in short supply. Since managers are trustees of our economic resources, the manager making this commitment cannot take it lightly.

FOOTNOTES

CHAPTER I

[1] Daniel Bell, *The Cultural Contradictions of Capitalism* (New York: Basic Books Inc., 1976); Michael Harrington, *Socialism* (New York: Saturday Review Press, 1972); John K. Galbraith, *Economics and the Public Purpose* (Boston: Houghton, Mifflin Company, 1973); Henry Fairlie, *The Spoiled Child of the Western World: The Miscarriage of the American Idea in Our Time* (Garden City: Doubleday and Company, 1976); George Lodge, *The New American Ideology* (New York: Alfred A. Knopf, 1975); Robert Nisbet, *The Twilight of Authority* (New York: Oxford University Press, 1975); Martin Mayer, *Today and Tomorrow in America* (New York: Harper and Row, 1976); Ralph Nader, Mark Green and Joel Seligman, *Taming the Giant Corporation* (New York: W. W. Norton and Company, 1976).

[2] Peter F. Drucker, *Management: Tasks, Responsibilities and Practices* (New York: Harper and Row, 1974), p. 8.

[3] ———, "The Embattled Businessman," *Newsweek*, February 16, 1976, p. 57.

CHAPTER II

[1] Israel M. Kirzner, *Competition and Economic Development* (Chicago: University of Chicago Press, 1973), pp. 26-27.

[2] Peter Kilby, ed., *Entrepreneurship and Economic Development* (New York: The Free Press, 1971), p. 2.

[3] Arthur H. Cole, "An Approach to the Study of Entrepreneurship," *Journal of Economic History*, 1946, VI, Supplement, p. 3.

[4] James H. Stauss, "The Entrepreneur: The Firm," *Journal of Political Economy*, LII, June 1944, p. 112.

[5] Joseph A. Schumpeter, *The Theory of Economic Development* (Cambridge, Mass.: Harvard University Press), 1936 p. 66.

[6] Joseph A. Schumpeter, *Business Cycles: A Theoretical, Historical and Statistical Analysis of the Capitalistic Process* Vol I (New York: McGraw-Hill, 1939), p. 84.

[7] Joseph A. Schumpeter, *Capitalism, Socialism and Democracy* (New York: Harper and Brothers, 1962), pp. 59-165.

[8] William J. Baumol, "Entrepreneurship in Economic Theory," *American Economic Review*, 58 (May 1968), p. 64.

[9] Joel Dean, *Managerial Economics* (New York: Prentice Hall, 1961); Robert Anthony, *Management Accounting Principles* (Homewood, Ill.: Richard D. Irwin, 1970); Edith T. Penrose, *The Theory and Growth of the Firm* (Oxford: Blackwell, 1959); Neil Chamberlain, *The Firm: Micro-Economic Planning and Action* (New York: McGraw-Hill, 1962); Ezra Solomon and John J. Pringle, *An Introduction to Financial Management* (Santa Monica, Calif.: Goodyear Publishing Company, Inc., 1977).

[10] Cole, *op. cit.*, pp. 3-4.

[11] David Clarence McClelland, *The Achieving Society* (Princeton, N.J.: Van Nostrand, 1962); Thomas C. Cochran, *The American Business System* (Cambridge, Mass.: Harvard University Press, 1957); Everett Hagan, *On the Theory of Social Change: How Economic Growth Begins* (Homewood, Ill.: The Dorsey Press Inc., 1962); Fritz Redlich, "The Origin of the Concepts of Entrepreneur and 'Creative Entrepreneurs' " in *Explorations in Entrepreneurial History*, 1, No. 2 (1953-1954), pp. 297-303.

[12] Schumpeter, *Theory of Economic Development*, p. 10.

[13] *Ibid.*, p. 93.

[14] Frank J. Knight, *Risk, Uncertainty and Profit* (New York: Houghton Mifflin Co., 1921), pp. 310-311.

[15] G. L. S. Shackle, *Decision, Order and Time in Human Affairs* (Cambridge: Cambridge University Press, 1969); ———, *Expectations, Enterprise and Profits* (London: Allen and Unwin, 1970).

[16] Knight, *op. cit.*, pp. 310-311.

[17] *Ibid.*, p. 268.

[18] Shackle, *Decision, Order and Time*, p. 67.

[19] G. L. S. Shackle, "Expectation and Liquidity," in *Expectations, Uncertainty and Behavior*, Mary Jean Bowman, ed. (New York: Social Science Research Council, 1958), p. 30.

[20] Shackle, *Expectations, Enterprise and Profits*, p. 148.

[21] Drucker, *Tasks*, pp. 506-516.

[22] Oskar Morgenstern, *On the Accuracy of Economic Observations* (Princeton, N.J.: Princeton University Press, 1963), p. 80.

[23] Ezra Solomon, *The Theory of Financial Management* (New York: Columbia University Press, 1963), pp. 15-20.

[24] Peter F. Drucker, *The New Society: The Anatomy of the Indus-*

trial Order (New York, Harper and Row, 1950); ———, *Managing for Results: Economic Tasks and Risk Taking Decisions* (New York: Harper and Row, 1964); ———, *The Age of Discontinuity: Guidelines to Our Changing Society* (New York: Harper and Row, 1968).

[25] Peter F. Drucker, "The Delusion of 'Profits,'" *The Wall Street Journal*, February 5, 1975.

[26] Robert N. Anthony, "The Trouble with Profit Maximization," *Harvard Business Review*, XXXVIII (November-December, 1960), p. 126.

[27] Solomon, *Theory of Financial Management*, p. 20.

[28] Reginald H. Jones, "Financing Our Future: The Challenge of Capital Formation," December 6, 1974, Address to: Conrress of Industry, National Association of Manufacturers, privately published by General Electric, p. 3.

[29] Drucker, *Tasks*, p. 125.

[30] Eugen Boehm-Bawerk, *The Positive Theory of Capital* translated by William Smart (New York: G. E. Stechert and Co., 1891), pp. 92-99.

[31] *Ibid.*, p. 99.

[32] *Ibid.*, pp. 237-248.

[33] Charles O. Hardy, *Risk and Risk Bearing* (Chicago: University of Chicago Press, 1923), p. 3.

[34] Theodore Levitt, *Innovation in Marketing: New Perspectives for Profit and Growth* (New York: McGraw-Hill Company Inc., 1962), p. 46.

[35] Drucker, *Managing for Results*, pp. 206-208.

[36] Leonard Silk, *The Economists* (New York: Basic Books, Inc., Publishers, 1976), pp. 137-138, 171, 198.

CHAPTER III

[1] Charles Alvin Dailey, *Entrepreneurial Management: Going All Out for Results* (New York: McGraw-Hill, 1971), p. 33.

[2] Ross J. Hoffman and Paul Levack, eds., *Selected Writings and Speeches of Edmund Burke* (New York: Alfred A. Knopf, 1949), p. 290.

[3] Fritz Machlup, *The Production and Distribution of Knowledge in the United States* (Princeton, N.J.: Princeton University Press, 1962), p. 362.

[4]———, "The Dropouts," *Forbes 50th Anniversary Issue*, September 15, 1967, p. 152.

[5]———, *The Confessions of St. Augustine* (New York: The Modern Library, 1949), p. 258.

[6]Ernest Holsendolph, "Think Tanks Have Sprung a Leak," *The New York Times*, January 9, 1977.

[7]Schumpeter, *Theory of Economic Development*, p. 9.

[8]Neil W. Chamberlain, *Enterprise and Environment: The Firm in Time and Place* (New York: McGraw-Hill, 1968), p. 9.

[9]Donald A. Schon, *Beyond the Stable State* (New York: Random House, 1971), pp. 31-61.

[10]Theodore Levitt, *The Marketing Mode: Pathways to Corporate Growth* (New York: McGraw-Hill, 1969), p. 1.

[11]Eric Hoffer, *Reflections on the Human Condition* (New York: Harper and Row, 1973), p. 68.

[12]Edwin A. Gee and Chaplin Tyler, *Managing Innovation* (New York: John Wiley and Sons, 1976), p. 105.

[13]Drucker, *Tasks*, p. 44.

[14]W. Paul Strassman, *Risk and Technological Innovation: American Manufacturing Methods During the Nineteenth Century* (Ithaca, New York: Cornell University Press, 1956), p. 211.

[15]Gilbert K. Chesterton, *Orthodoxy* (New York: John Lane Company, 1908), p. 148.

[16]Kirzner, *op. cit.*, p. 68.

[17]Eric Hoffer, *The Passionate State of Mind* (New York: Harper and Row, 1954), p. 109.

[18]Levitt, *Marketing Mode*, pp. 97-98.

CHAPTER IV

[1]C. J. Slaybaugh, "Pareto's Law and Modern Management," *Price, Waterhouse Review* (Winter, 1966), pp. 26-33.

[2]Drucker, *Managing for Results*, pp. 27-37.

[3]Philip Kotler, "Phasing Out Weak Products," *Harvard Business Review*, Vol. 43 (March-April 1965), p. 109.

[4]George J. Stigler, *Essays in the History of Economics* (Chicago: The University of Chicago Press, 1965), p. 109.

[5]Samuel Enoch Stumpf, *Socrates to Sartre: A History of Philosophy* (New York: McGraw-Hill, 1966), p. 94.

[6]Peter J. Schuyten, "How MCA Discovered Movieland's Golden Lode," *Fortune*, November, 1976.

[7]Drucker, *Tasks*, pp. 46-47.
[8]Theodore Levitt, "The Industrialization of Service," *Harvard Business Review* (September-October, 1976), p. 68.
[9]Lewis Mumford, *Techniques and Civilization* (New York: Harcourt Brace and Company, 1934), pp. 12-18.
[10]———, "The Breakdown of U.S. Innovation," *Business Week*, February 16, 1976.
[11]Levitt, *Marketing Mode*, pp. 28-53; ———, "Exploiting the Product Life Cycle," *Harvard Business Review*, Vol. 43, pp. 81-94.
[12]Philip Kotler, *Marketing Management* (Englewood Cliffs, N.J.: Prentice Hall, 1972), p. 436.
[13]Abraham H. Maslow, *Toward a Psychology of Being* (Princeton, N.J.: D. Van Nostrand Company Inc., 1962), p. 23.
[14]Peter F. Drucker, "Why Consumers Aren't Behaving," *The Wall Street Journal*, December 11, 1976.
[15]Questions were framed chiefly from the following sources: John F. Childs, *Profit Goals and Capital Management* (Englewood Cliffs, N.J.: Prentice Hall, 1968); ———, *Earnings Per Share and Management Decisions* (Englewood Cliffs, N.J.: Prentice Hall, 1972); Peter Drucker, "Aftermath of the Go-Go Decade," *The Wall Street Journal*, March 25, 1975; ———, "Managing Capital Productivity," *The Wall Street Journal*, July 24, 1975; ———, "Six Durable Economic Myths," *The Wall Street Journal*, September 16, 1975.
[16]Drucker, *Managing for Results*, pp. 212-216.

CHAPTER V

[1]C. Northcote Parkinson, *Parkinson's Law* (Boston: Houghton Mifflin Company, 1957); Laurence J. Peter and Raymond Hull, *The Peter Principle* (New York: William Morrow, 1969); Anthony Jay, *Management and Machiavelli: An Inquiry into the Politics of Corporate Life* (New York: Holt, Rinehart and Winston, 1968); Robert Townsend, *Up the Organization* (New York: Alfred J. Knopf, 1970).
[2]J. Samuel Bois, *Breeds of Men: Toward the Adulthood of Mankind* (New York: Harper and Row, 1969), pp. 91-92.
[3]B. F. Skinner, *Beyond Freedom and Dignity* (New York: Alfred A. Knopf, 1971).
[4]Harry Levinson, *The Exceptional Executive: A Psychological Conception* (Cambridge, Mass.: Harvard University Press, 1968), pp. 27-29.
[5]Abraham H. Maslow, *Motivation and Personality* (New York:

Harper and Row Publishers, 1970), p. 35.

[6]*Ibid.*, p. 59.

[7]Saul Gellerman, *Management by Motivation* (New York: American Management Association Inc., 1968), pp. 187-203.

[8]Frederick Herzberg, *Work and the Nature of Man* (Cleveland: The World Publishing Company, 1966), pp. 95-96.

[9]*Ibid.*, pp. 82-86; Frederick Herzberg, Bernard Mausner, and Barara Snyderman, *The Motivation To Work* (New York: John Wiley and Sons, Inc., 1967), pp. 59-83.

[10]Herzberg, *Work and the Nature of Man,* p. 170.

[11]*Ibid.*, p. 78.

[12]Douglas McGregor, *The Human Side of Enterprise* (New York: McGraw-Hill Company, 1960), pp. 33-45.

[13]Chris Argyris, *Personality and Organization: The Conflict Between the System and the Organization* (New York: Harper and Brothers, 1957), p. 233.

[14]Chris Argyris, "The Integration of the Individual and the Organization," in *Social Science Approaches to Business Behavior*, George B. Strother, ed. (Homewood, Ill.: The Dorsey Press Inc., 1962), p. 75.

[15]William Glasser, *Reality Therapy: A New Approach to Psychiatry* (New York: Harper and Row, 1965), p. 193.

[16]Skinner, *op. cit.*, p. 40.

[17]William T. Powers, *Behavior: The Control of Perception* (Chicago: Aldine, 1973), p. 259.

[18]John J. Tarrant, *Drucker: The Man Who Invented the Corporate Society* (Boston: Cahners Book Inc., 1976), p. 260.

[19]Drucker, *Tasks*, pp. 243-244.

[20]Adam Bruno Ulam, *The Fall of the University* (New York: Library Press, 1973).

[21]Morris Bishop, *Blaise Pascal* (New York: Dell Publishing Co. Inc., 1966), p. 202.

[22]George Odiorne, *Management and the Activity Trap* (New York: Harper and Row), pp. 64-77; James Cribbin, *Effective Managerial Leadership* (New York: American Management Association, 1972), p. 152.

CHAPTER VI

[1]Stauss, *op. cit.*, p. 112.

[2]Alfred D. Chandler, Jr., *Strategy and Structure* (Cambridge, Mass.: M.I.T. Press, 1962).

Footnotes

[3] Peter F. Drucker, *The Effective Executive* (New York: Harper and Row, 1967), pp. 9-16.
[4] Victor Papanek, *Design for the Real World: Human Ecology and Social Change* (New York: Pantheon Books, 1971), p. 230.
[5] Drucker, *Tasks*, pp. 638-639.
[6] I am indebted to Mr. Henry Boettinger of the American Telephone and Telegraph Company for introducing me to this formula.
[7] Drucker, *Tasks*, p. 412-414.
[8] Walter Kaufmann, ed., *Philosophic Classics: Thales to Saint Thomas* (Englewood Cliffs, N.J.: Prentice Hall, 1961), p. 65.
[9] Louise Hall Tharp, *Until Victory: Horace Mann and Mary Peabody* (Boston: Little, Brown and Company, 1953), p. 161.
[10] ———, *The Confessions of Saint Augustine*, p. 256.
[11] *Ibid.*, p. 258.
[12] R. Alec MacKenzie, *The Time Trap* (New York: American Management Association, 1972); James T. McCay, *The Management of Time* (Englewood Cliffs, N.J.: Prentice Hall, 1958); Alan Lakein, *How to Get Control of Your Time and Your Life* (New York: Peter H. Wydon, 1973); Joseph D. Cooper, *How to Get More Done in Less Time* (New York: Doubleday and Company, 1952).
[13] William Shakespeare, *The Tragedy of Hamlet: The Prince of Denmark*, edited by Tucker Brooke and Jack Randall Crawford (New Haven: Yale University Press, 1954), Act. IV, Scene III, p. 143.
[14] ———, *The Maxims of LaRochefoucauld*, translated by Louis Kronenberger (New York: Random House, 1959), p. 128.
[15] Forrest C. Pogue, *George C. Marshall, Education of a General 1880-1939*, Vol. I (New York: The Viking Press, 1963), p. 278.
[16] Drucker, *Effective Executive*, p. 86.
[17] William James, *Talks to Teachers: And to Students On Some of Life's Ideals* (New York: Henry Holt and Company, 1929), p. 65.
[18] Kaufmann, *op. cit.*, p. 68.

BIBLIOGRAPHY

1. Books

Anthony, Robert. *Management Accounting Principles*. Homewood, Ill.: R. D. Irwin, 1970.

Argyris, Chris. "The Integration of the Individual and the Organization," in *Social Sciences Approaches to Business Behavior*. George B. Struther, ed. Homewood, Ill.: The Dorsey Press, Inc., 1962.

———. *Personality and Organization: The Conflict Between the System and the Organization*. New York: Harper and Brothers, 1957.

Bell, Daniel. *The Cultural Contradictions of Capitalism*. New York: Basic Books Inc., 1976.

Bishop, Morris. *Blaise Pascal*. New York: Dell Publishing Co., Inc., 1966.

Boehm-Bawerk, Eugene V. *The Positive Theory of Capital*. Translated by William Smart. New York: G. E. Stechert and Co., 1891.

Bois, J. Samuel. *Breeds of Men: Toward the Adulthood of Mankind*. New York: Harper and Row, 1969.

Bowman, M. J. *Expectations, Uncertainty and Business Behavior*. New York: Social Science Research Council, 1958.

Chamberlain, Neil W. *Enterprise and Environment: The Firm in Time and Place*. New York: McGraw-Hill, 1968.

———. *The Firm: Micro-Economic Planning and Action*. New York: McGraw-Hill, 1962.

Chandler, Alfred D., Jr. *Strategy and Structure*. Cambridge, Mass.: M.I.T. Press, 1962.

Chesterton, Gilbert K. *Orthodoxy*. New York: John Lane Co., 1909.

Childs, John F. *Earnings Per Share and Management Decisions*. Englewood Cliffs, N.J.: Prentice-Hall, 1971.

———. *Profit Goals and Capital Management*. Englewood Cliffs, N.J.: Prentice-Hall, 1968.

Cochran, Thomas C. *The American Business System: A Historical Perspective, 1900-1955*. Cambridge, Mass.: Harvard University Press, 1957.

———. *The Inner Revolution: Essays in the Social Sciences in History*. New York: Harper and Row, 1964.

Cooper, Joseph D. *How to Get More Done in Less Time*. New York: Doubleday and Company, 1952.

Cribbin, James. *Effective Managerial Leadership*. New York: American Management Association, 1972.

Dailey, Charles A. *Entrepreneurial Management: Going All Out for Results*. New York: McGraw-Hill, 1971.

Dean, Joel. *Managerial Economics*. New York: Prentice-Hall, 1951.

Drucker, Peter. *The Age of Discontinuity: Guidelines to Our Changing Society*. New York: Harper and Row, 1968.

———. *The Effective Executive*. New York: Harper and Row, 1967.

———. *Management: Tasks, Responsibilities and Practices*. New York: Harper and Row, 1974.

———. *Managing for Results: Economic Tasks and Risk-Taking Decisions*. New York: Harper and Row, 1964.

———. *The New Society: The Anatomy of the Industrial Order*. New York: Harper, 1950.

Fairlie, Henry. *The Spoiled Child of the Western World: The Miscarriage of the American Idea in Our Time*. Garden City: Doubleday and Company, 1934.

Galbraith, John K. *Economics and the Public Purpose*. Boston: Houghton Mifflin Co., 1973.

Gee, Edwin and Tyler, Chaplin. *Managing Innovation*. New York: John Wiley and Sons, 1976.

Gellerman, Saul. *Management by Motivation*. New York: American Management Association, 1968.

Glasser, William. *Reality Therapy: A New Approach to Psychiatry*. New York: Harper and Row, 1965.

Hagan, Everett. *On the Theory of Social Change: How Economic Growth Begins*. Homewood, Ill.: The Dorsey Press, 1962.

Hardy, Charles O. *Risk and Risk Bearing*. Chicago: University of Chicago Press, 1923.

Harrington, Michael. *Socialism*. New York: Saturday Review Press, 1972.

Herzberg, Frederick, Mausner, Bernard, and Snyderman, Barbara. *The Motivation to Work*. New York: John Wiley and Sons Inc., 1967.

Herzberg, Frederick. *Work and the Nature of Man*. Cleveland: The World Publishing Company, 1966.

Hoffer, Eric. *The Passionate State of Mind*. New York: Harper and Row 1954.

———. *Reflections on the Human Condition*. New York: Harper and Row, 1973.

Bibliography

Hoffman, Ross, and Levack, Paul, eds. *Selected Writings and Speeches of Edmund Burke*. New York: Alfred A. Knopf, 1949.

James, William. *Talks to Teachers: And to Students on Some of Life's Ideals*. New York: Henry Holt and Co., 1929.

Jay, Anthony. *Management and Machiavelli: An Inquiry into the Politics of Corporate Life*. New York: Holt, Rinehart, and Winston, 1968.

Kaufman, Walter, ed. *Philosophic Classics: Thales to Saint Thomas*. Englewood Cliffs, N.J.: Prentice-Hall, 1961.

Kilby, Peter, ed. *Entrepreneurship and Economic Development*. New York: The Free Press, 1971.

Kirzner, Israel M. *Competition and Economic Development*. Chicago: University of Chicago Press, 1973.

Knight, F. J. *Risk, Uncertainty and Profit*. New York: Houghton Mifflin Co., 1921.

Kotler, Philip. *Marketing Management*. Englewood Cliffs, N.J.: Prentice-Hall, 1972.

Lakein, Alan. *How to Get Control of Your Time and Your Life*. New York: Peter H. Wyden, 1973.

Levinson, Harry. *The Exceptional Executive: A Psychological Conception*. Cambridge, Mass.: Harvard University Press, 1968.

Levitt, Theodore. *Innovation in Marketing: New Perspectives for Profit and Growth*. New York: McGraw-Hill, 1962.

──────. *The Marketing Mode: Pathways to Corporate Growth*. New York: McGraw-Hill, 1969.

Lodge, George. *The New American Ideology*. New York: Alfred A. Knopf, 1975.

Machlup, Fritz. *The Production and Distribution of Knowledge in the United States*. Princeton, N.J.: Princeton University Press, 1962.

MacKenzie, R. Alec. *The Time Trap*. New York: American Management Association, 1972.

Maslow, Abraham H. *Motivation and Personality*. New York: Harper and Row Publishers, 1970.

──────. *Toward A Psychology of Being*. Princeton, N.J.: D. Van Nostrand Company Inc., 1962.

Mayer, Martin. *Today and Tomorrow in America*. New York: Harper and Row, 1976.

McCay, James T. *The Management of Time*. Englewood Cliffs, N.J.: Prentice-Hall, 1958.

McClelland, David. *The Achieving Society*. Princeton, N.J.: D. Van Nostrand Company Inc., 1961.

McGregor, Douglas. *The Human Side of Enterprise*. New York: McGraw-Hill, 1960.
Morgenstern, Oskar. *On the Accuracy of Economic Observations*. Princeton, N.J.: Princeton University Press, 1963.
Mumford, Lewis. *Technics and Civilization*. New York: Harcourt, Brace and Company, 1934.
Nader, Ralph, Green, Mark and Seligman, Joel. *Taming the Giant Corporation*. New York: W. W. Norton and Company, 1976.
Nisbet, Robert. *The Twilight of Authority*. Oxford: Oxford University Press, 1975.
Papanek, Victor. *Design for the Real World: Human Ecology and Social Change*. New York: Pantheon Books, 1971.
Parkinson, Northcote C. *Parkinson's Law*. Boston: Houghton Mifflin Company, 1957.
Penrose, E. T. *The Theory and Growth of the Firm*. New York: John Wiley and Sons, 1959.
Peter, Lawrence J. and Hull, Raymond. *The Peter Principle*. New York: William Morrow, 1969.
Pogue, Forrest C. *George C. Marshall: Education of a General 1880-1939*, Vol. 1. New York: The Viking Press, 1963.
Powers, William T. *Behavior: The Control of Perception*. Chicago: Aldine Publishing Company, 1973.
Schon, Donald A. *Beyond the Stable State*. New York: Random House, 1971.
Schumpeter, Joseph A. *Business Cycles: A Theoretical, Historical and Statistical Analysis of the Capitalistic Process*, Vol. 1. New York: McGraw-Hill, 1939.
―――. *Capitalism, Socialism, and Democracy*. New York: Harper and Brothers, 1962.
―――. *The Theory of Economic Development*. Cambridge, Mass.: Harvard University Press, 1936.
Shackle, G. L. S. *Decision, Order and Time in Human Affairs*. Cambridge, Mass.: Cambridge University Press, 1969.
―――. *Expectations, Enterprise and Profits*. London: Allen and Unwin, 1970.
―――. "Expectation and Liquidity" in *Expectations, Uncertainty and Behavior*. Mary Jean Bowman, ed. New York: Social Science Research Council, 1958.
Shakespeare, William. *The Tragedy of Hamlet: The Prince of Denmark*, edited by Tucker Brooke and Jack Randall. Crawford, New Haven: Yale University Press, 1954.

Bibliography

Silk, Leonard. *The Economists*. New York: Basic Books Inc., 1976.

Skinner, B. F. *Beyond Freedom and Dignity*. New York: Alfred A. Knopf, 1971.

Solomon, Ezra and Pringle, John J. *An Introduction to Financial Management*. Santa Monica, Calif.: Goodyear Publishing Co., Inc., 1977.

Solomon, Ezra. *The Theory of Financial Management*. New York: Columbia University Press, 1963.

Stigler, George J. *Essays in the History of Economics*. Chicago: University of Chicago Press, 1965.

Strassman, W. Paul. *Risk and Technological Innovation: American Manufacturing Methods During the Nineteenth Century*. Ithaca, New York: Cornell University Press, 1956.

Stumpf, Samuel Enoch. *Socrates to Sarte: A History of Philosophy*. New York: McGraw-Hill, 1966.

Tarrant, John J. *Drucker: The Man Who Invented the Corporate Society*. Boston: Cahners Books Inc., 1976.

Tharp, Louise Hall. *Until Victory: Horace Mann and Mary Peabody*. Boston: Little, Brown and Company, 1953.

Townsend, Robert. *Up the Organization*. New York: Alfred A. Knopf, 1970.

Ulam, Adam Bruno. *The Fall of the American University*. New York: The Library Press, 1973.

―――. *The Confessions of Saint Augustine*, translated by Edward B. Pusey. New York: The Modern Library, 1949.

―――. *The Maxims of LaRochefoucauld*, translated by Louis Kronenberger. New York: Random House, 1959.

2. Articles

Anthony, Robert N. "The Trouble with Profit Maximization," *Harvard Business Review*, Vol. 38 (November-December, 1960), pp. 126-134.

Baumol, W. J. "Entrepreneurship in Economic Theory," *American Economic Review*, Vol. 58 (May, 1968), pp. 64-71.

Cole, Arthur H. "An Approach to the Study of Entrepreneurship," *Journal of Economic History*, Vol. VI (Supplement, 1946), pp. 1-15.

Drucker, Peter, "Aftermath of a Go-Go Decade," *The Wall Street Journal*, 18:4 (March 25, 1975).

―――. "The Delusion of Profits," *The Wall Street Journal*, 10:4 (February 5, 1975).

———. "Managing Capital Productivity," *The Wall Street Journal*, 12:3 (July 24, 1975).

———. "Six Durable Economic Myths," *The Wall Street Journal*, 26:4 (September 16, 1975).

———. "Why Consumers Aren't Behaving," *The Wall Street Journal*, 20:4 (December 1, 1975).

Holsendolph, Ernest. "Think Tanks Have Sprung a Leak," *The New York Times* (January 9, 1977).

Jones, Reginald H. "Financing Our Future: The Challenge of Capital Formation," (December 6, 1974), speech published by General Electric, pp. 1-4.

Kotler, Philip. "Phasing Out Weak Products," *Harvard Business Review*, Vol. 43 (March-April, 1965), pp. 107-118.

Levitt, Theodore. "Exploiting the Product Life Cycle," *Harvard Business Review*, Vol. 43 (November-December, 1965), pp. 81-94.

———. "The Industrialization of Service," *Harvard Business Review*, Vol. 54 (September-October, 1976), pp. 63-74.

Redlich, Fritz. "The Origin of the Concepts of Entrepreneur and 'Creative Entrepreneur,' " in *Explorations in Entrepreneurial History*, Vol. 1, No. 2 (1953-1954), pp. 297-303.

Schuyten, Peter J. "How MCA Discovered Movieland's Golden Lode," *Fortune* (November, 1976).

Stauss, James H. "The Entrepreneur: The Firm," *Journal of Political Economy*, Vol. LII (June, 1944), pp. 112-127.

Slaybaugh, C. J. "Pareto's Law and Modern Management," *Price, Waterhouse Review* (Winter, 1966), pp. 26-33.

———. "The Breakdown of U.S. Innovation," *Business Week* (February 16, 1976).

———. "The Dropouts," *Forbes 50th Anniversary Issue* (September 15, 1967), pp. 50-55.

———. "The Embattled Businessman," *Newsweek* (February 16, 1976).

INDEX

Adams, John Quincy, 148
Alcoa, 50, 94
Allstate, 43
American Telephone and Telegraph, 58, 67-71, 78, 83
Anheuser-Busch, 49, 74-75
Anthony, Robert, 14, 25
Argyris, Chris, 108, 118-119
Atlantic and Pacific, 46, 86
Avery, Sewall, 25-26
Axiologically Good, 119
Axiologically Good Organization, 119

Baumol, William J., 13-14
Bell Labs, 58, 67, 125
Bell System, 58, 67, 69, 70
Bernovilli, Daniel, 86
Bernovilli, Theorem, 86, 87
Boehm-Bawerk, Eugene, 29-30
Bois, J. Samuel, 109
Boulding, Kenneth, 36
Buick, 61
Bulova, 94
Burke, Edmund, 37
Bush, Vanevaar, 63
Business Cycles, 12

Cadillac, 61
Cambell's Soup, 49
Cantillon, Richard, 11
Capitalism, Socialism, and Democracy, 13
Carterfone Ruling, 70
Chamberlain, Neil, 14, 45
Chamfort, Sebastian, 110
Chandler, Alfred, 128
Chesterton, Gilbert K., 59
Chevrolet, 61
Chrysler, 87
Clausen, A. W., 7
Coca-Cola, 50, 95

Cochran, Thomas C., 17
Columbia Broadcasting System, 53
Communications Act of 1934, 68
Consumer Communications Reform Act, 70
Coors, 99
Coty, 77

Dailey, Charles, 37
Dean, Joel, 14
Democritus, 141, 151
De Soto, 87
Drago, 88
Drucker, Peter F., 23, 101, 120
Du Pont, 94, 128

Economics and the Public Purpose, 4
Edison, Thomas A., 55
Edsel, 61, 87
Emile, 120
Engel's Law, 99

Fairchild, 94
Fairlie, Henry, 4
Federal Communication Commission, 70-71
Fels, 96
Ford Motor Company, 30, 61, 87
Ford, Henry I., 30, 64
Ford, Henry II, 30
Francis, Clarence, 149
Freud, Sigmund, 112, 113
Friedman, Milton, 36
Frost, Robert, 146

Galbraith, John K., 4, 36
Galileo, 55
Gantt, H. L., 57
Gellerman, Saul, 115
General Electric, 28, 35, 38, 43, 50, 66, 83, 94, 128
General Foods, 49, 98, 99, 149
General Motors, 44, 66, 99, 128
Gerber Foods, 49

Index

Gilette, 34
Glasser, William, 119
Grant, W. T., 86
Green, Mark, 4

Hagan, Everett, 17
Hardy, Charles O., 31-32
Harrington, Michael, 4
Heilbroner, Robert, 10
Herzberg, Frederick, 108, 115-116
Hoffer, Eric, 55, 62
Hoover, Herbert, 148
House of Branfi, 57
Hunt Foods, 85
Huxley, Julian, 137

International Business Machines, 43, 50, 69, 94
International Chemical, 49

James, William, 150
Jay, Anthony, 109
Jones, Reginald, 28

Kaiser, 94
Kelvin, Lord William Thomson, 55
Kettering, Charles, 66
Kimberly Clark, 50
King Solomon, 130
Kirzner, Israel, 10, 60
Knight, Frank, 19-20
Kotler, Philip, 97
Kresge K Mart, 86

Lafayette National Bank, 77
Land, Edwin H., 94
La Rochefoucauld, 147
Lavoisier, 55
Leacock, Stephen, 150
Leahy, Admiral, 55
Lee Myles, 88
Leontief, Wassily, 36

Levinson, Harry, 113
Levitt, Theodore, 33, 48, 91
Lincoln, Abraham, 62, 148
Lodge, George, 4

Ma Bell, 93
MCA, 88
Management By Motivation, 115
Manhattan Project, 55, 62
Mann, Horace, 142, 143
Marshall, Alfred, 11
Marshall, General George, 148
Marks and Spencer, 48
Marx, Karl, 11, 103
Maslow, Abraham, 99, 108, 113-114
Maslow's Hierarchy Theory, 99-100
Maytag, 50
Mayer, Martin, 4
McClellan, David, 17
McDonald's, 48
McGregor, Douglas, 108, 116-118
Midas, 88
Miller, 99
Morgenstern, Oskar, 23
Motivation and Personality, 113
Mumford, Lewis, 93
Murphy's Law, 133, 143

Nabisco, 34, 49
Nader, Ralph, 4-5
Newcomb, Simon, 55
Newton's Law, 141
New York Telephone Company, 54
Nisbet, Robert, 4

Occam, William of, 87
Occam's Law, 87
Occam's Razor, 87
Oldsmobile, 61
Owen, Robert, 11

Index

Pabst, 99
Pareto, Vilfredo, 77
Pareto's Law, 77, 78, 80, 92, 101
Pareto's Principle, 79, 80
Parkinson, C. Northcote, 109, 142
Parkinson's Law, 105
Pascal, Blaise, 121
Pavlov, Ivan, 111
Penney, J. C., 49
Penrose, Edith T., 14
Pepsi, 95
Peter, Laurence, 109
Plato, 150
Polaroid, 91, 94
Pontiac, 61
Powers, William T., 120
Priestly, J. B., 55
Pringle's Potato Chips, 40
Proctor and Gamble, 40

RCA, 38, 83
Rashomon Effect, 46
Rayco 88
Redlich, Fritz, 17
Revlon, 48
Revlon, Charles, 48-49
Reynolds, 94
Rickey, Branch, 151
Risk and Risk Bearing, 31
Riunite Wine, 57,
Roentgen, 55
Rosenwald, Julius, 42
Rousseau, Jean Jacques, 62, 120, 121
Rutherford, Lord Ernest, 55

Saint Augustine, 39, 143
Saint Simon, Henri de, 11
Samuelson, Paul, 36
Say, Jean Baptiste, 11, 15, 16
Schlitz, 99
Schon, Donald, 46

Schopenhauer, 144
Schumpeter, Joseph A., 12-13, 17, 43
Scott, 49
Sears, Richard, 42
Sears Roebuck, 42-43, 48, 80 94, 105, 128
Seligman, Joel, 4
Seven-Eleven, 80, 81, 92
Shackle, G.L.S., 13, 19-22
Shakespeare, William, 146
Silk, Leonard, 36
Skinner, B. F., 111
Sloan, Alfred, 100, 152
Smith, Adam, 25
Socialism; 4
Solomon, Ezra, 14, 23-24, 27
Standard Oil, 128
Stanky, Eddie, 151
Stauss, James H., 11, 125
Steele, Albert, 95

Taming The Giant Corporation, 4
Texas Instruments Company, 83, 94
The Confessions of St. Augustine, 39, 143
The Cultural Contradiction of Capitalism, 4
The Human Side of Enterprise, 117
The New American Ideology, 4
The Spoiled Child of the Western World, 4
The Theory of Economic Development, 12
The Twilight of Authority, 4
Thomson, D'Arcy, 137
Three M, 66-67, 98, 104
Today and Tomorrow in America, 4
Toward a Psychology of Being, 113
Townsend, Robert, 109
Truman, Harry, 133, 148

Ulam, Adam Bruno, 121
United States Steel, 43, 52, 94
Universal Studios, 89

Vail Theodore, 68-69, 152

Index

Wasserman, Lew, 88, 89
Watson, John, 111
Wells, H. G., 56
Western Electric, 67
Westinghouse, 35, 38
Wieser's Principles of Continuity, 43
Wood, General Robert, 43, 152
Wright Brothers, 55

Xerox, 65, 136

Yankelovitch, Daniel, 6